GRAPHIC MODERN HISTORY: COLD WAR CONFLICTS

THE CUBAN MISSILE CRISIS

By Gary Jeffrey & Illustrated by Terry Riley

Crabtree Publishing Company
www.crabtreebooks.com

Crabtree Publishing Company

www.crabtreebooks.com

1-800-387-7650

Publishing in Canada
616 Welland Ave.
St. Catharines, ON
L2M 5V6

Published in the United States
PMB 59051, 350 Fifth Ave.
59th Floor,
New York, NY

Printed in Hong Kong/092013/BK20130703

Copyright © **2013 David West Children's Books**

Created and produced by:

David West Children's Books

Project development, design, and concept:

David West Children's Books

Author and designer: Gary Jeffrey

Illustrator: Terry Riley

Editors: Lynn Peppas,

Kathy Middleton

Proofreader: Kelly McNiven

Project coordinator:

Kathy Middleton

Production coordinator and

Prepress technician:

Ken Wright

Print coordinator:

Margaret Amy Salter

Photographs:

p4t, p5t, Library of Congress;
p44t, C.I.A.; p45m, p47, John F.
Kennedy Presidential Library
and Museum

Library and Archives Canada Cataloguing in Publication

Jeffrey, Gary, author
        The Cuban Missile Crisis / by Gary Jeffrey and
illustrated by Terry Riley.

(Graphic modern history : Cold War conflicts)
Includes index.
Issued in print and electronic formats.
ISBN 978-0-7787-1233-6 (bound).--ISBN 978-0-7787-1237-4
(pbk.).--ISBN 978-1-4271-9344-5 (pdf).--ISBN 978-1-4271-9340-7
(html)

        1. Cuban Missile Crisis, 1962--Juvenile literature.
2. Cuban Missile Crisis, 1962--Comic books, strips, etc. 3 .
Cuba--History--Invasion, 1961--Juvenile literature. 4. Cuba--
History--Invasion, 1961--Comic books, strips, etc. 5. Cuba--
History--Revolution, 1959--Comic books, strips, etc. 6. Cuba--
History--Revolution, 1959--Juvenile literature. 7. Graphic
novels. I. Riley, Terry, illustrator II. Title. III. Series: Jeffrey,
Gary. Graphic modern History. Cold War conflicts

F1788.J35 2013   j972.9106'4   C2013-904128-1
                                              C2013-904129-X

Library of Congress Cataloging-in-Publication Data

Jeffrey, Gary, author.
 The Cuban Missile Crisis / by Gary Jeffrey and illustrated by
Terry Riley.
        p. cm. -- (Graphic modern history : cold war conflicts)
 Includes index.
 ISBN 978-0-7787-1233-6 (reinforced library binding) -- ISBN
978-0-7787-1237-4 (pbk.) -- ISBN 978-1-4271-9344-5 (electronic
pdf) -- ISBN 978-1-4271-9340-7 (electronic html)
1. Cuban Missile Crisis, 1962--Comic books, strips, etc. 2.
Cuban Missile Crisis, 1962--Juvenile literature. 3. Cuba--
History--Revolution, 1959--Comic books, strips, etc. 4. Cuba--
History--Revolution, 1959--Juvenile literature. 5. Cuba--
History--Invasion, 1961--Comic books, strips, etc. 6. Cuba--
History--Invasion, 1961--Juvenile literature. 7. Graphic novels.
I. Riley, Terry, illustrator. II. Title.

E841.J44 2014
972.9106'4--dc23

                                              2013023907

CONTENTS

THE CUBAN REVOLUTION

At the end of World War II, the United States and the Soviet Union began a dangerous rivalry called the Cold War. The two countries did not battle each other directly, but competed instead to control or influence other countries.

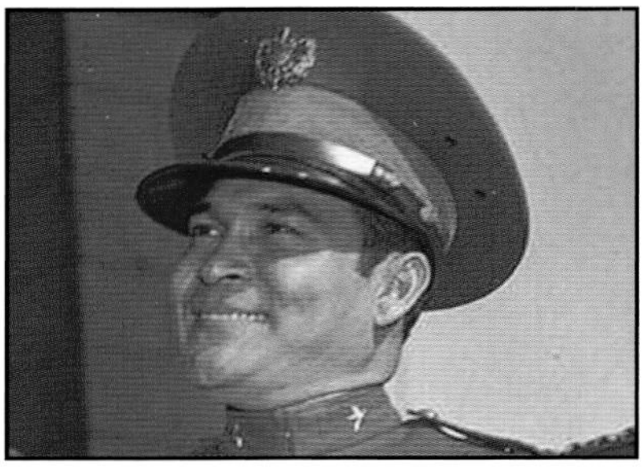

In 1938, Batista was head of the Cuban army.

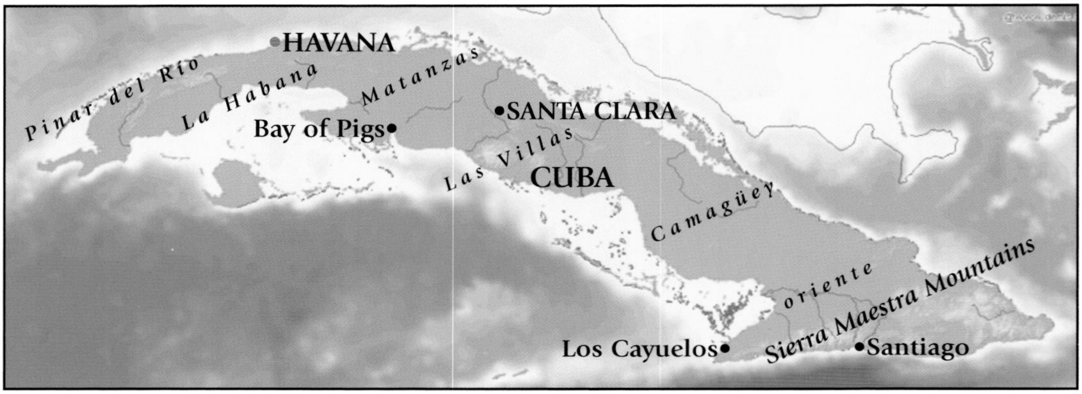
HAVANA
Pinar del Río
La Habana
Matanzas
Bay of Pigs
SANTA CLARA
Las Villas
CUBA
Camagüey
oriente
Sierra Maestra Mountains
Los Cayuelos
Santiago

A former Spanish colony, Cuba is the largest of the Caribbean Islands. It became independent in 1902.

Master of the Coup

From the beginning of the Cold War in 1947, the United States was determined to stop the spread of communism. The U.S. government supported a series of dictators that would help them keep communism out of their backyard. One of these dictators was Fulgencio Batista, who had led a revolt in 1933 in Cuba. For seven years, Batista ruled as army chief behind a series of puppet, or powerless, presidents. Elected president himself in 1940, his government lasted one term.

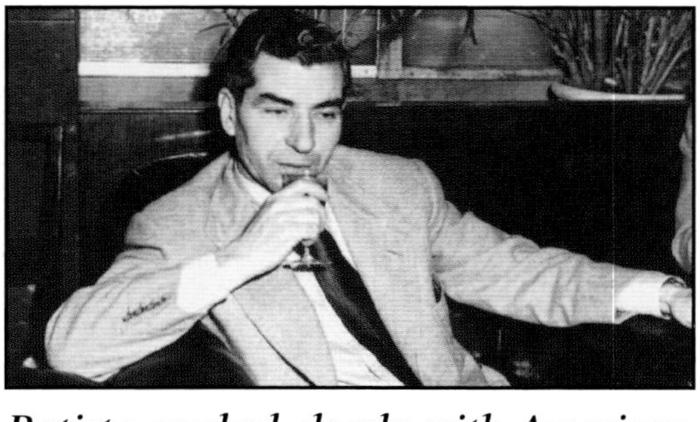

Batista worked closely with American mobsters like "Lucky" Luciano.

He moved to the United States but returned to Cuba to run in the 1952 election. But Batista used the army to stage a coup instead and set himself up as dictator. He served American interests, lined his own pockets, and repressed the poor.

The Revolutionaries

In 1953, 27-year-old lawyer Fidel Castro led a failed student revolt in Santiago, Cuba, and was jailed for two years. When he was released, he fled to Mexico in order to build a guerrilla army to overthrow the crooked Batista. In Mexico, he joined his brother Raúl and a young doctor from Argentina—Ernesto "Che" Guevara—who had himself witnessed the cruelty of dictatorships across central and South America. Castro began training soldiers and named their rebellion the 26th July Movement after the date of his first, failed revolt.

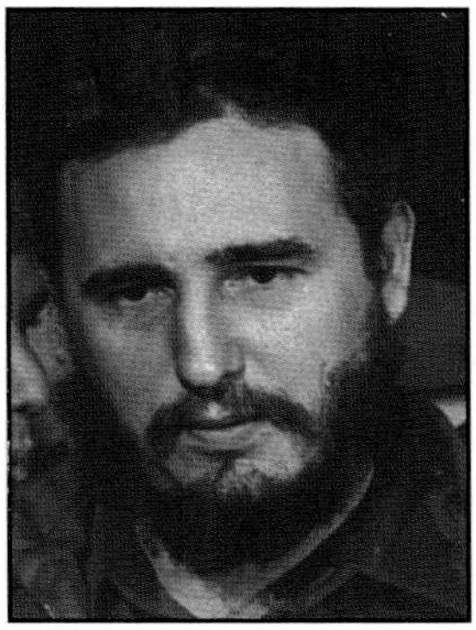

Fidel Castro believed that a revolution could topple Batista if it gained the support of the peasants of Cuba.

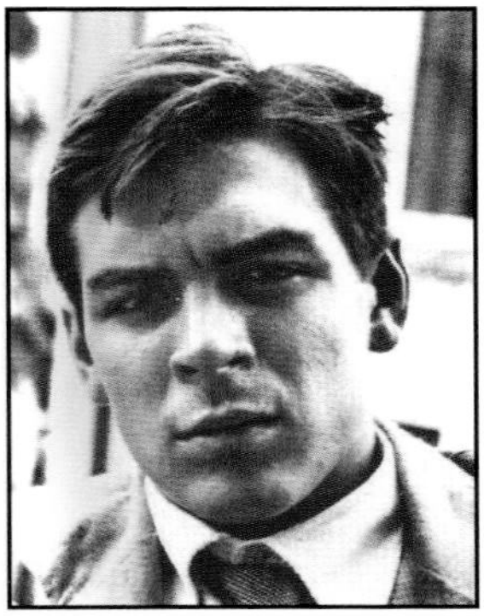

Traveling across Latin America had radicalized the young Ernesto Guevara.

Guerrilla War

Late in 1956, Castro sailed with 82 rebels by leaky boat to Los Cayuelos, Cuba. Batista's forces attacked quickly, leaving just 19 rebels remaining to set up camp in the Sierra Maestra Mountains.

The dense forest hid this core group and they began the work of winning the hearts and minds of the people of the Oriente province. Guevara became Castro's second-in-command. Guevara's mission was to advance the rebels into the important province of Las Villas. Batista dealt harshly with officers in his army and his demoralized men fought badly. Soon, Guevara's forces arrived at Santa Clara, winning the final battle for Cuba.

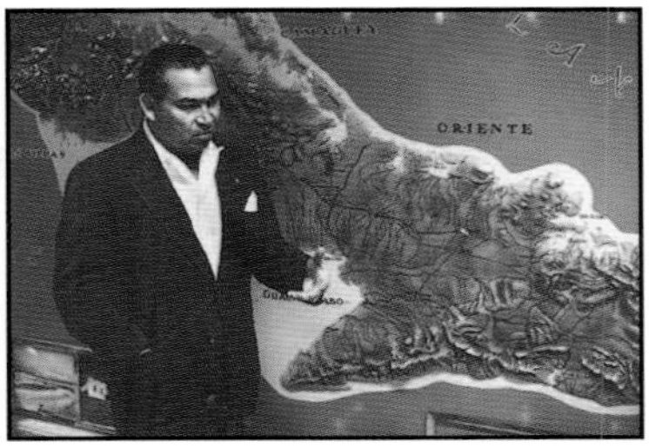
ORIENTE

In 1957 Batista was bent on stopping the revolution.

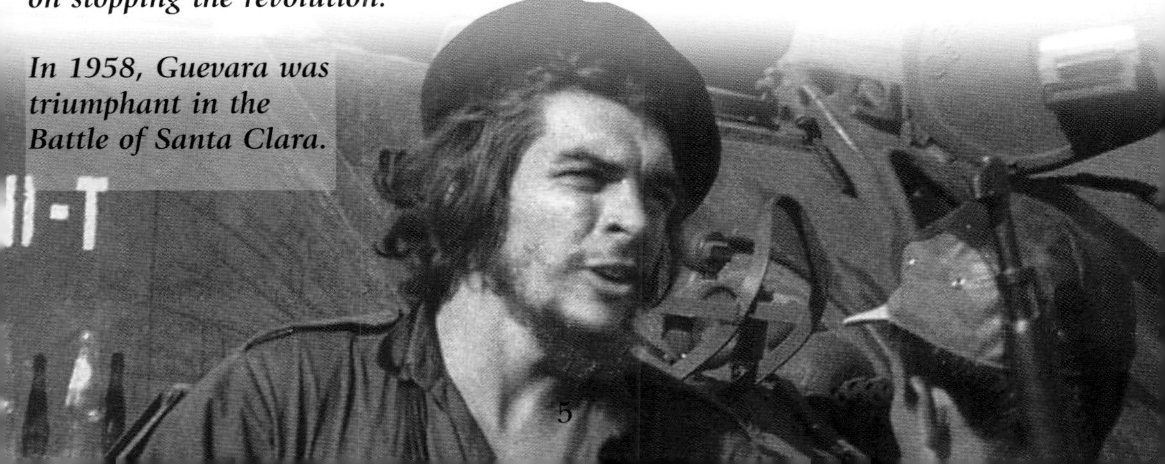

In 1958, Guevara was triumphant in the Battle of Santa Clara.

COUNTER REVOLUTION!

The revolutionaries took power on January 1, 1959, with Manuel Urrutia as president. Urrutia was considered a moderate who would be accepted by the powerful United States. People loyal to Batista were executed to make sure there would be no counterrevolution.

In 1959, Castro traveled to the United States and told them, "…very clearly we are not communists…"

SHARP LEFT TURN

Castro, as prime minister—and head of a growing militia—had strong ideas about the kind of society he wanted for Cuba. A Marxist, he was opposed to free elections. Urrutia disagreed with Castro and resigned. The United States grew concernd as Castro continued with executions and stamped out rival anti-Batista groups. Cuba was developing into an uncontrollable, single-party dictatorship and had begun talking to the Soviets—America's enemy.

The final straw came in 1960 when the Cuban government seized ownership of all Cuban industries, as well as all U.S.-owned land in Cuba. The United States cut diplomatic ties and began a trade embargo against Cuba—now seen as a potential enemy.

In 1954, CIA Director Allan Dulles had overseen a successful CIA-organized coup in Guatemala to protect U.S. business interests.

COVERT ACTION

In the United States, the Central Intelligence Agency (CIA) had been working on a secret plan to invade Cuba to set up a counter-revolutionary government. Operation Zapata was approved by U.S. President Eisenhower and later handed over to John F. Kennedy when he became president.

Fifteen hundred armed, CIA-trained Cuban exiles would land at Bahia de Cochinos (Bay of Pigs) to establish a beachhead. The plan was to set up a temporary government in Cuba quickly.

Air Strikes

The landing date was set for April 17, 1961. Two days before, eight (CIA-supplied) B26 planes disguised with Cuban Air Force (FAR) markings and piloted by Cuban exiles attacked airfields in Cuba. This was a signal to Castro that Cuban defectors would be supplying air power for the invasion.

In response Castro had thousands of people he suspected of being disloyal to the revolution rounded up and held in prison.

José "Pepe" San Román was the commander of the invasion force.

Disaster at the Bay of Pigs

Many things went wrong right away (see page 20). President Kennedy called off a dawn air strike against the Cuban Air Force because he did not want the United States to look like it was involved in the invasion. Castro's planes had control of the sky. He also had the overwhelming support of his people. The invasion force—Brigade 2506—fought hard, but they were outnumbered by more than 230,000 Cuban army, militia, and police, who killed 118 and captured 1,202 of the invaders.

Kennedy's refusal to allow the U.S. Navy or its aircraft to assist had sealed the brigade's fate. The Bay of Pigs failure led Castro to declare Cuba a communist country under the protection of the Soviet Union.

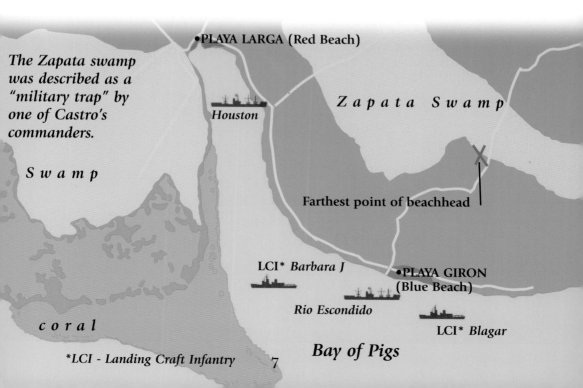

The Zapata swamp was described as a "military trap" by one of Castro's commanders.

•PLAYA LARGA (Red Beach)

Zapata Swamp

Houston

Swamp

Farthest point of beachhead

LCI* Barbara J

•PLAYA GIRON (Blue Beach)

Rio Escondido

coral

LCI* Blagar

*LCI - Landing Craft Infantry

Bay of Pigs

7

THE BATTLE OF SANTA CLARA

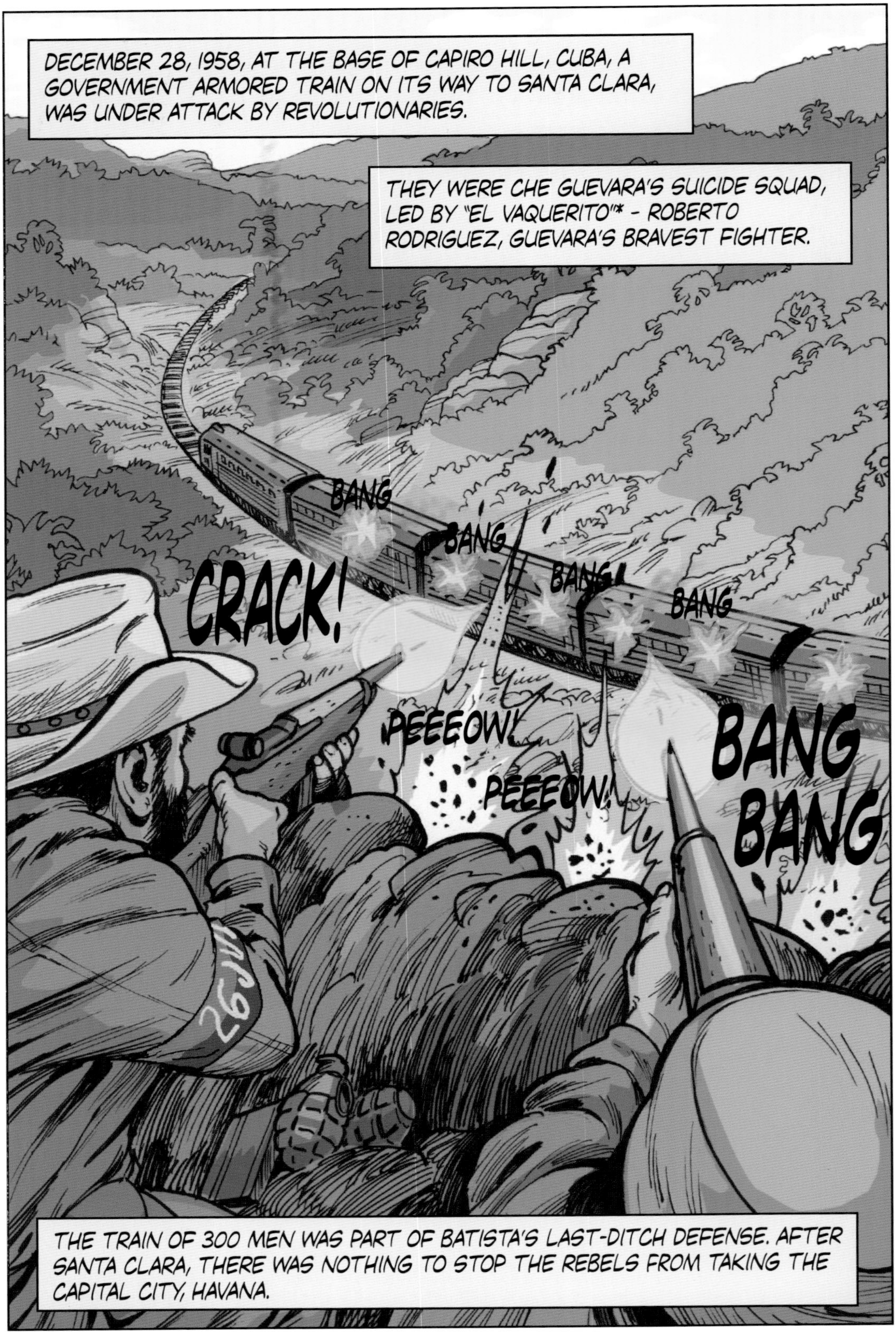
DECEMBER 28, 1958, AT THE BASE OF CAPIRO HILL, CUBA, A GOVERNMENT ARMORED TRAIN ON ITS WAY TO SANTA CLARA, WAS UNDER ATTACK BY REVOLUTIONARIES.
THEY WERE CHE GUEVARA'S SUICIDE SQUAD, LED BY "EL VAQUERITO"* - ROBERTO RODRIGUEZ, GUEVARA'S BRAVEST FIGHTER.
BANG
BANG
BANG
BANG
CRACK!
PEEEOW!
PEEEOW!
BANG BANG
THE TRAIN OF 300 MEN WAS PART OF BATISTA'S LAST-DITCH DEFENSE. AFTER SANTA CLARA, THERE WAS NOTHING TO STOP THE REBELS FROM TAKING THE CAPITAL CITY, HAVANA.

*"THE COWBOY"

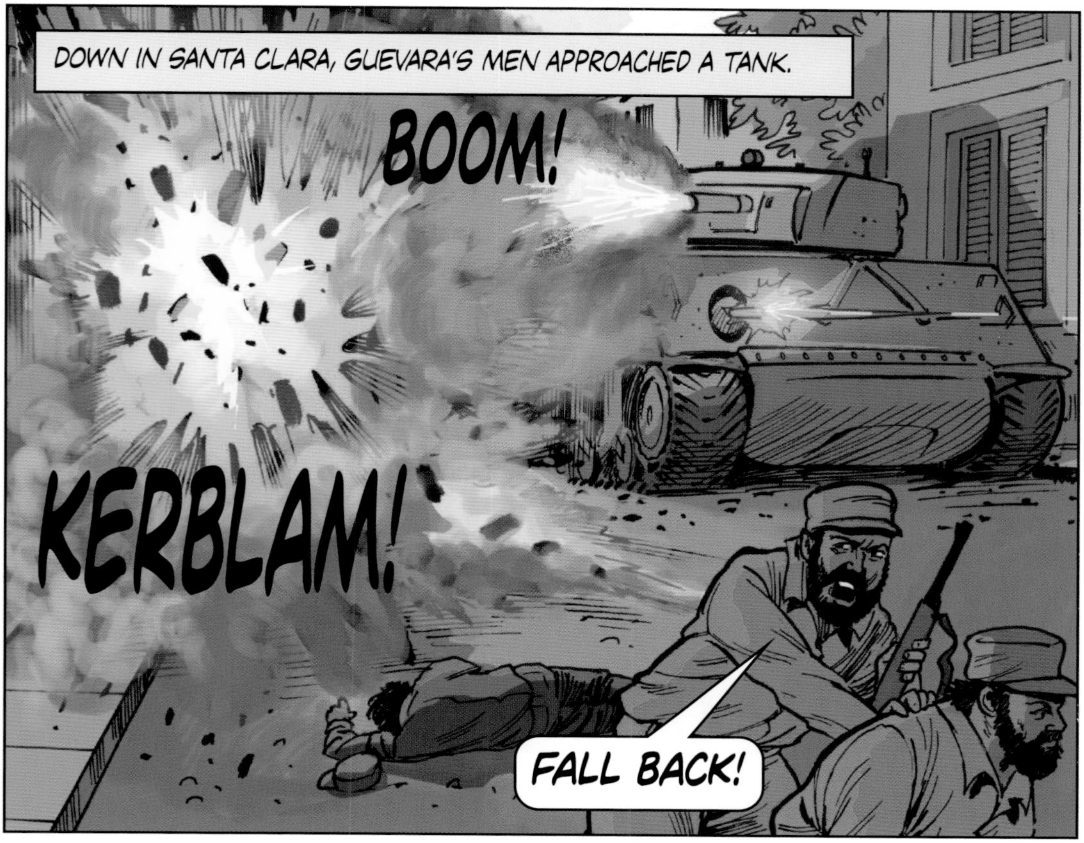
DOWN IN SANTA CLARA, GUEVARA'S MEN APPROACHED A TANK.
BOOM!
KERBLAM!
FALL BACK!

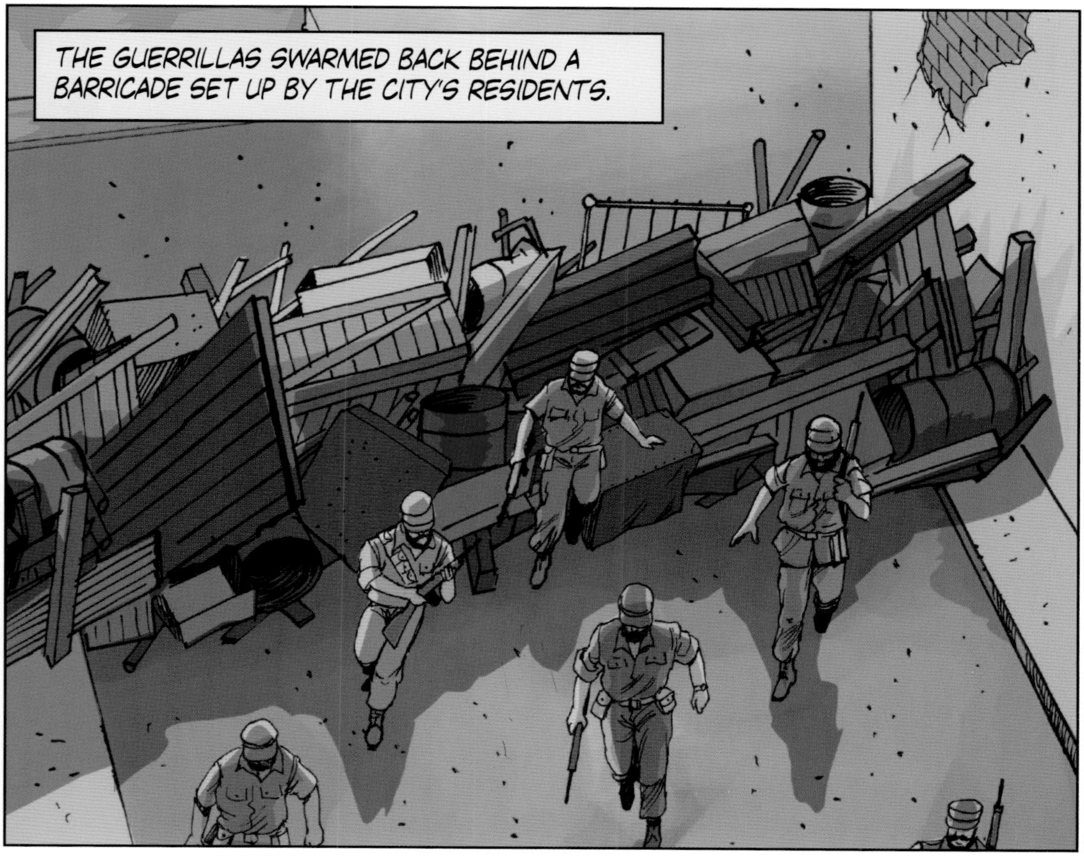
THE GUERRILLAS SWARMED BACK BEHIND A BARRICADE SET UP BY THE CITY'S RESIDENTS.

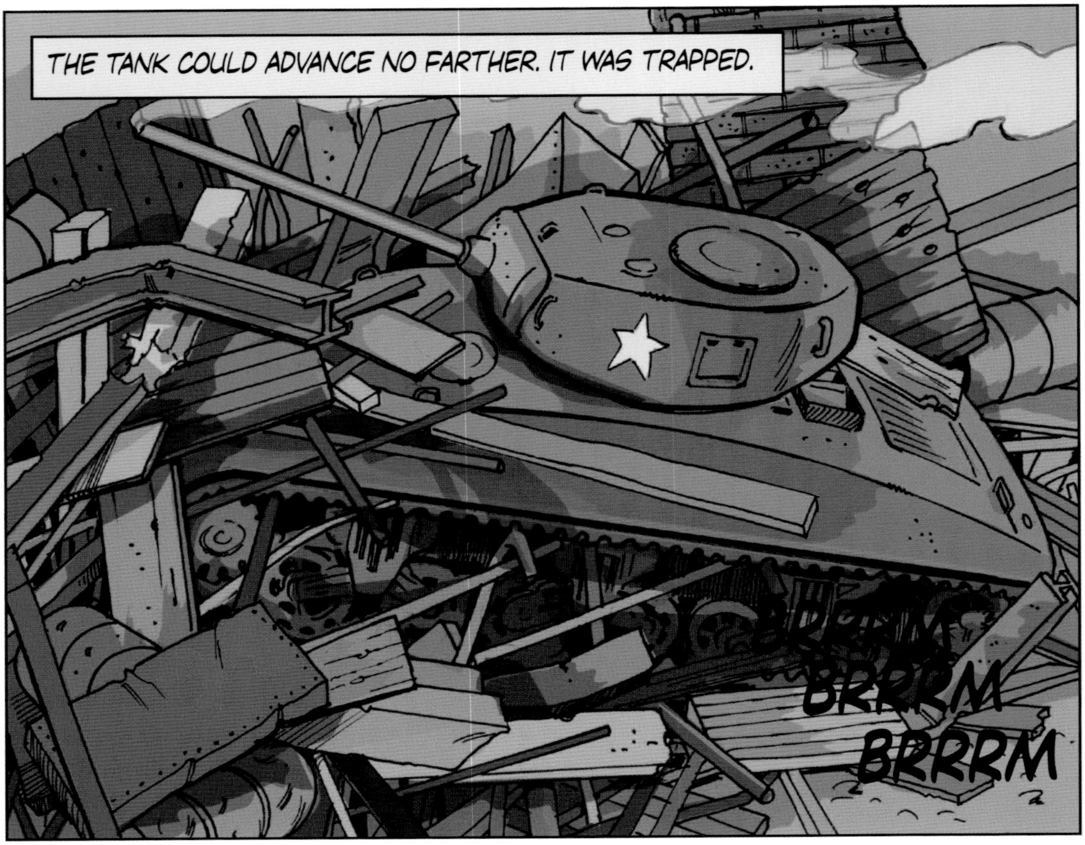
THE TANK COULD ADVANCE NO FARTHER. IT WAS TRAPPED.
BRRRM
BRRRM
BRRRM

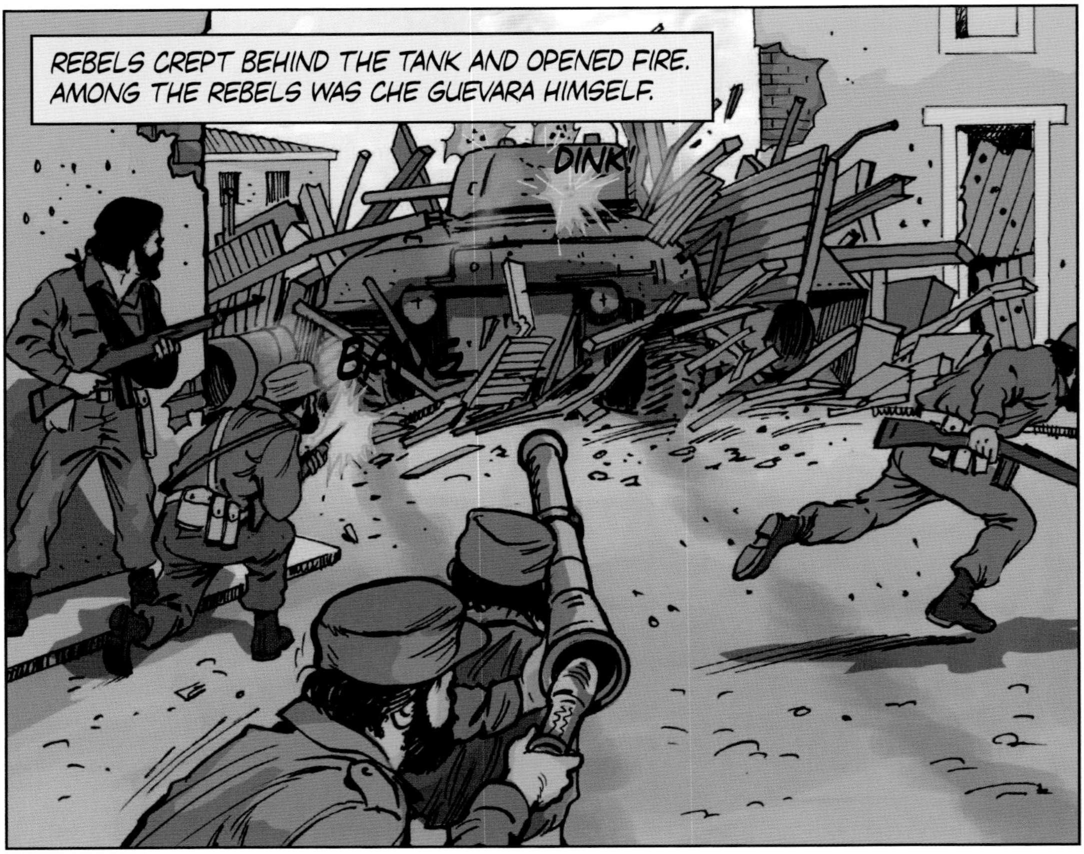
REBELS CREPT BEHIND THE TANK AND OPENED FIRE. AMONG THE REBELS WAS CHE GUEVARA HIMSELF.
DINK!

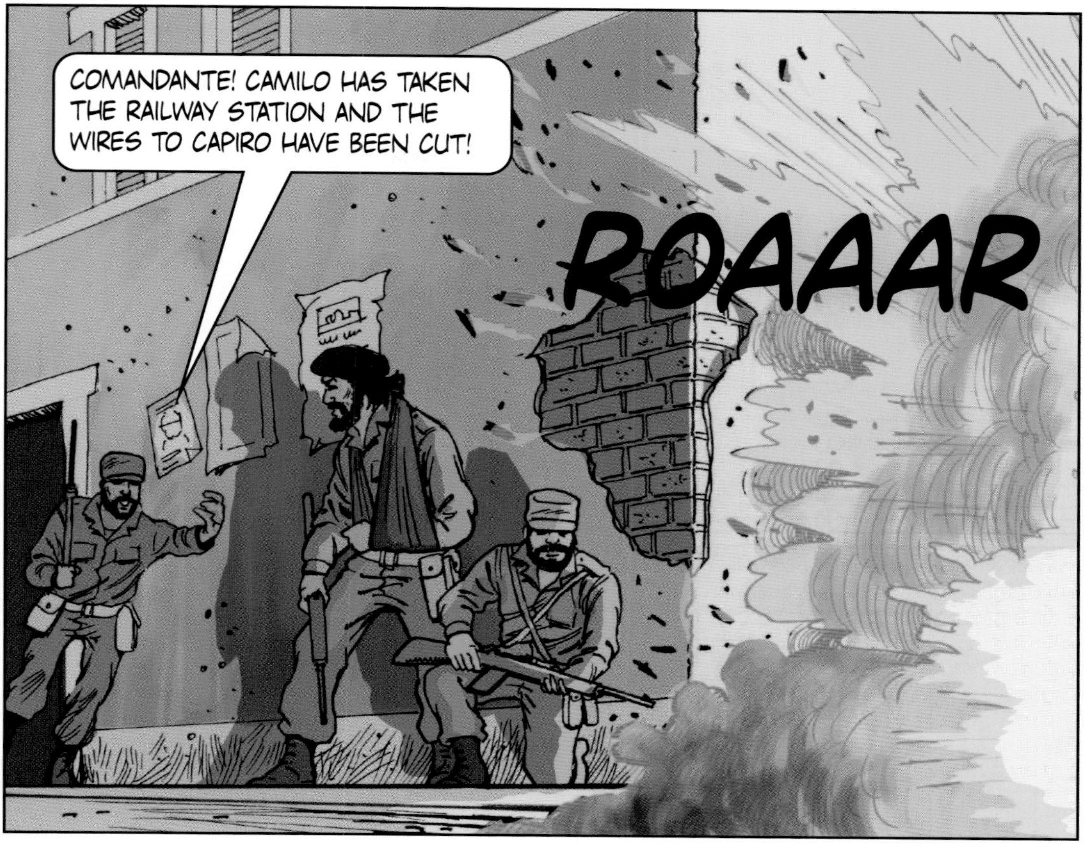
COMANDANTE! CAMILO HAS TAKEN THE RAILWAY STATION AND THE WIRES TO CAPIRO HAVE BEEN CUT!
ROAAAR

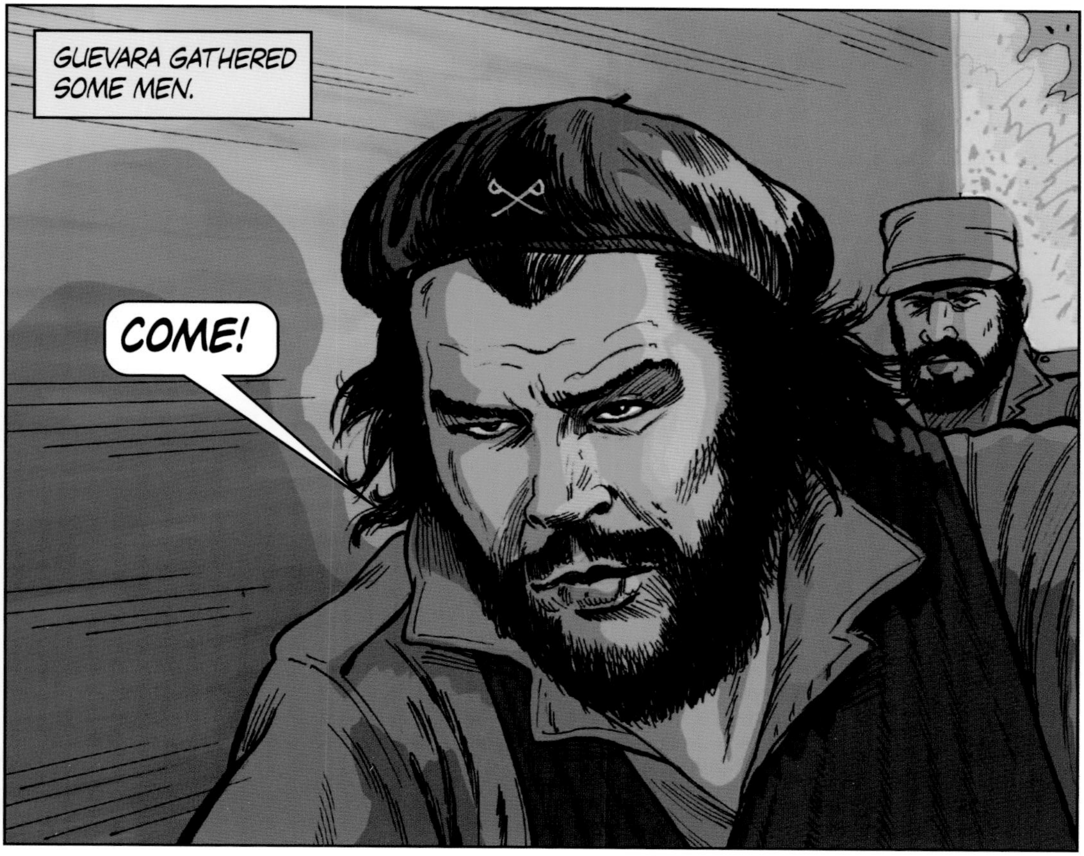
GUEVARA GATHERED SOME MEN.
COME!

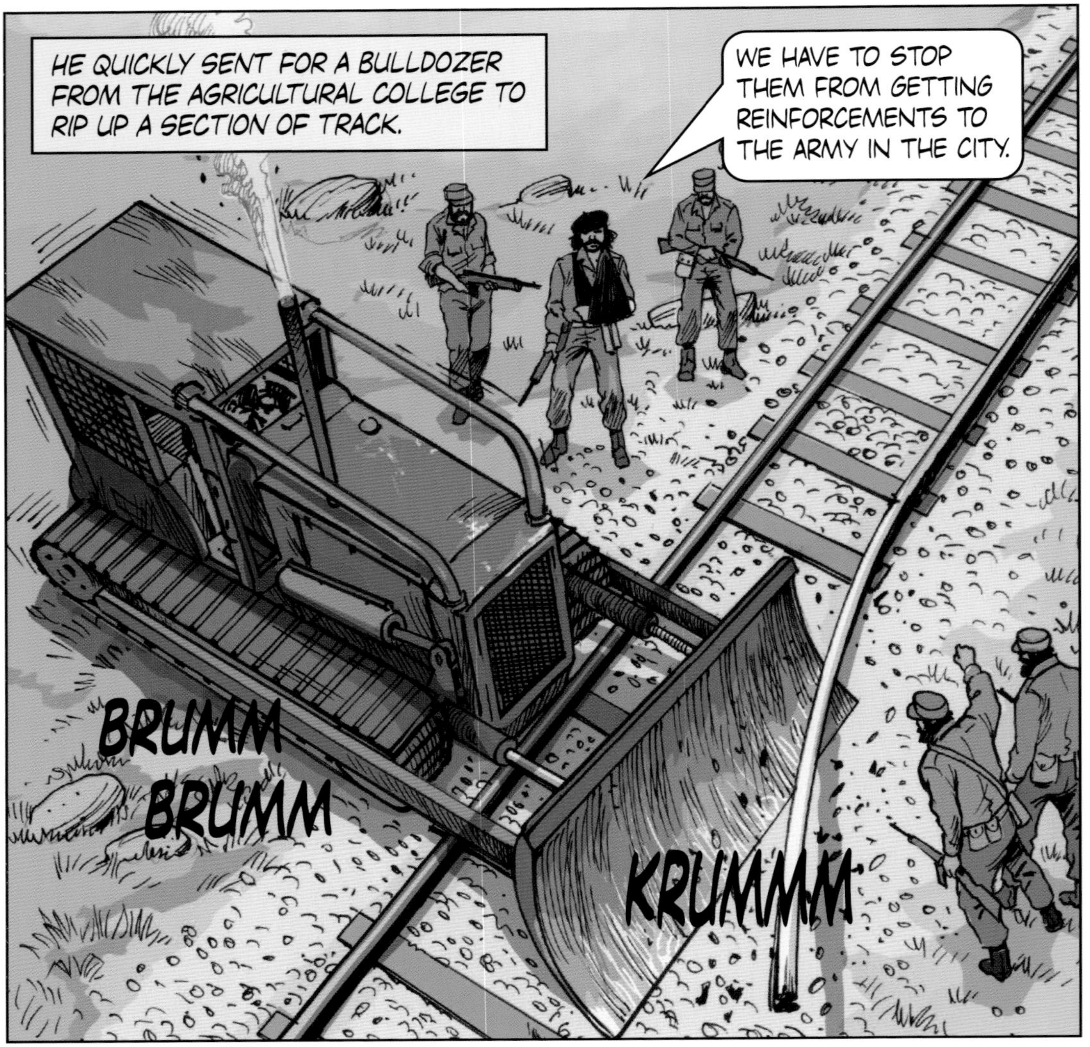
HE QUICKLY SENT FOR A BULLDOZER FROM THE AGRICULTURAL COLLEGE TO RIP UP A SECTION OF TRACK.
WE HAVE TO STOP THEM FROM GETTING REINFORCEMENTS TO THE ARMY IN THE CITY.
BRUMM BRUMM
KRUMMM

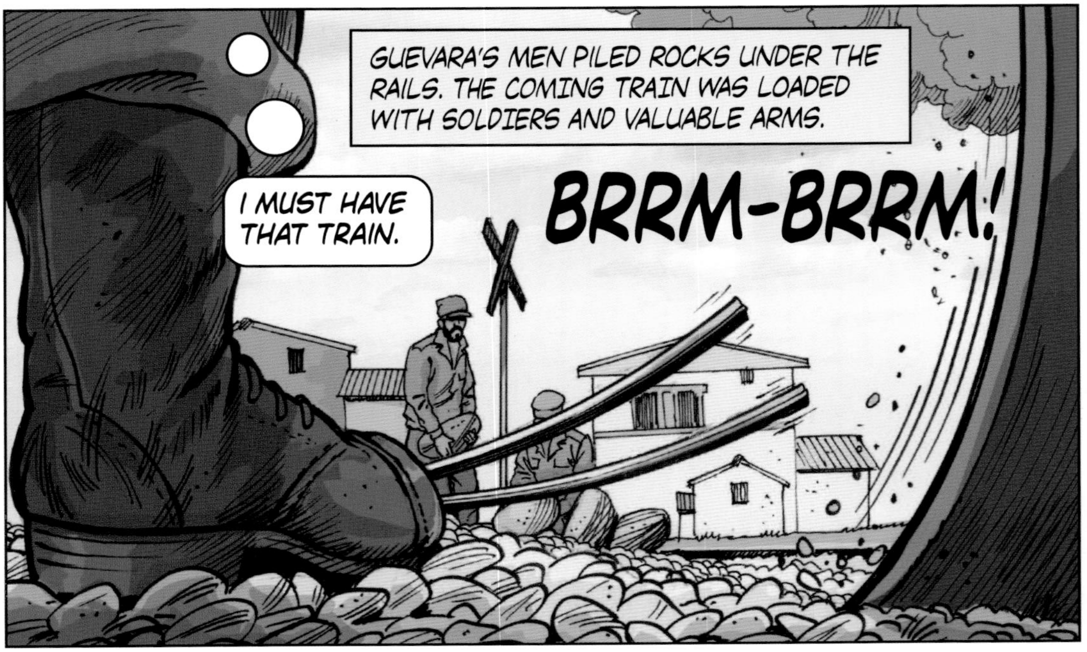
GUEVARA'S MEN PILED ROCKS UNDER THE RAILS. THE COMING TRAIN WAS LOADED WITH SOLDIERS AND VALUABLE ARMS.
I MUST HAVE THAT TRAIN.
BRRM-BRRM!

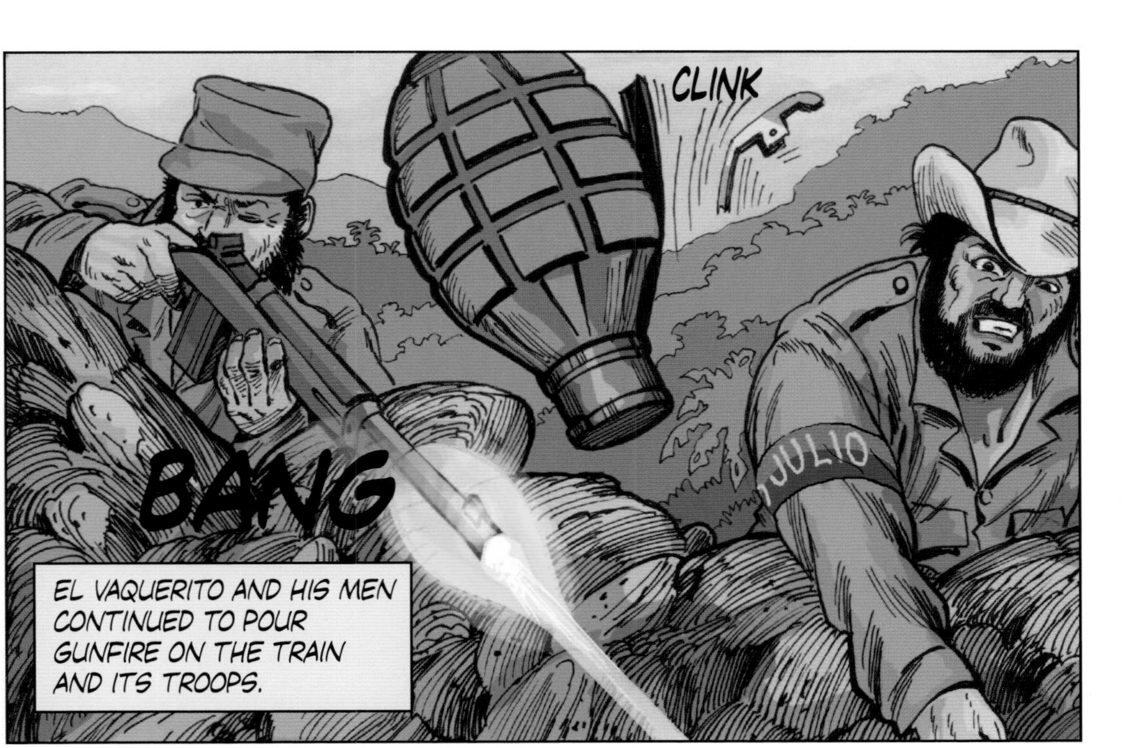
CLINK
BANG
JULIO
EL VAQUERITO AND HIS MEN CONTINUED TO POUR GUNFIRE ON THE TRAIN AND ITS TROOPS.

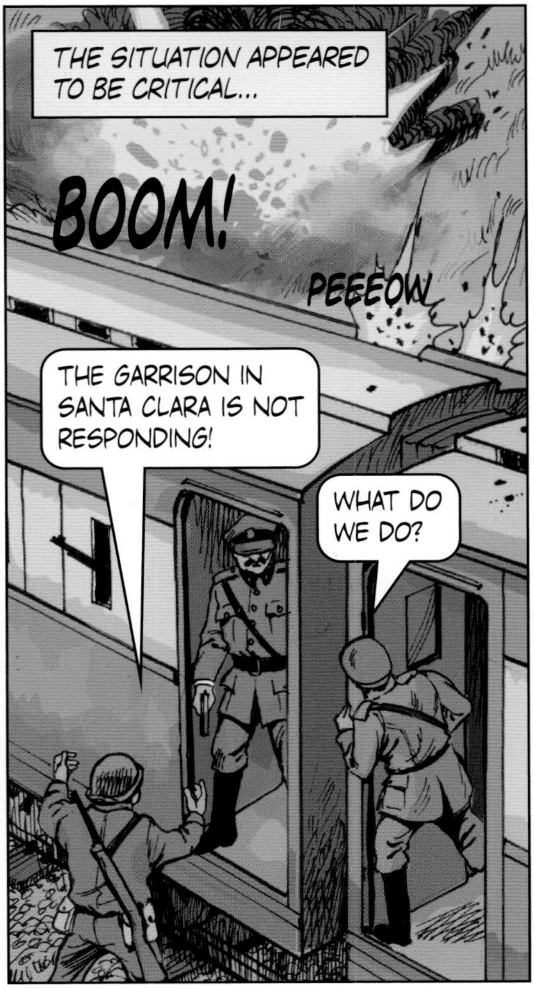
THE SITUATION APPEARED TO BE CRITICAL...
BOOM!
PEEEOW
THE GARRISON IN SANTA CLARA IS NOT RESPONDING!
WHAT DO WE DO?

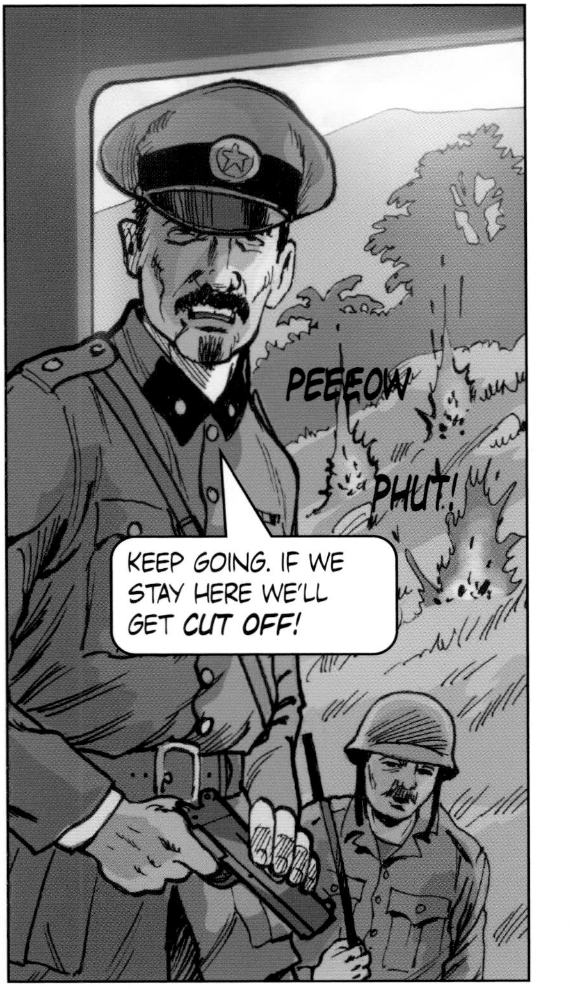
PEEEOW
PHUT!
KEEP GOING. IF WE STAY HERE WE'LL GET **CUT OFF!**

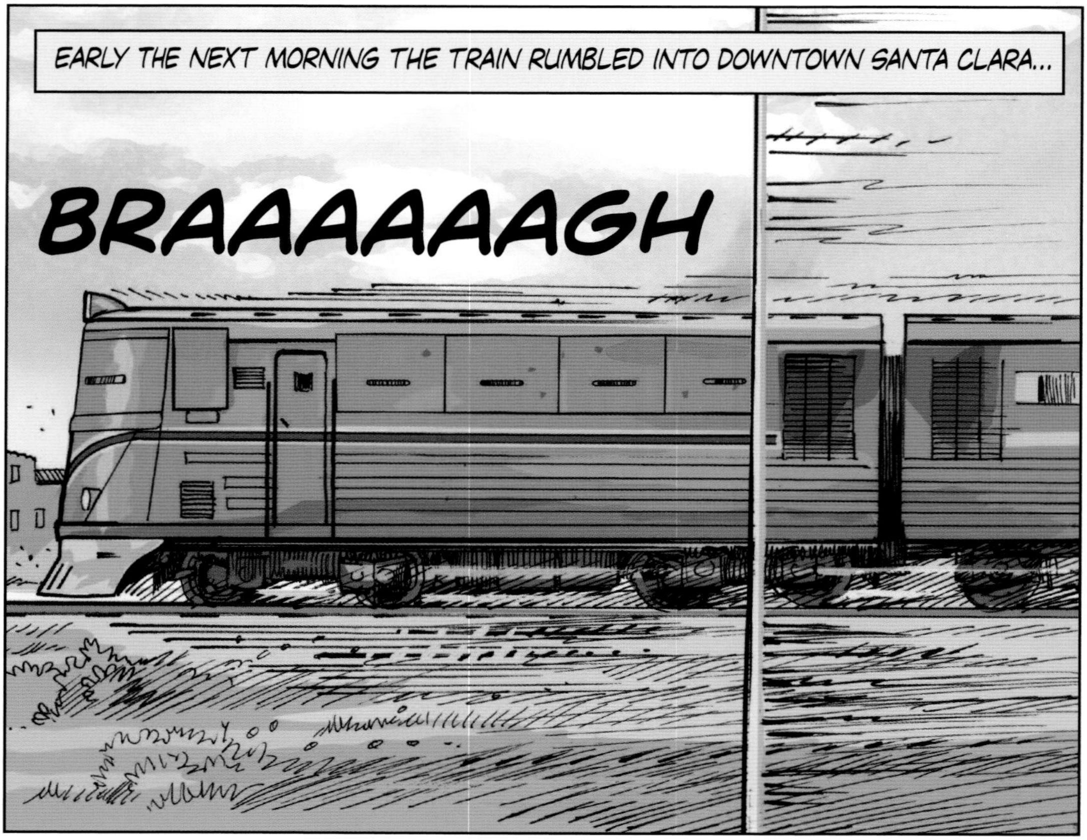
EARLY THE NEXT MORNING THE TRAIN RUMBLED INTO DOWNTOWN SANTA CLARA...
BRAAAAAAGH

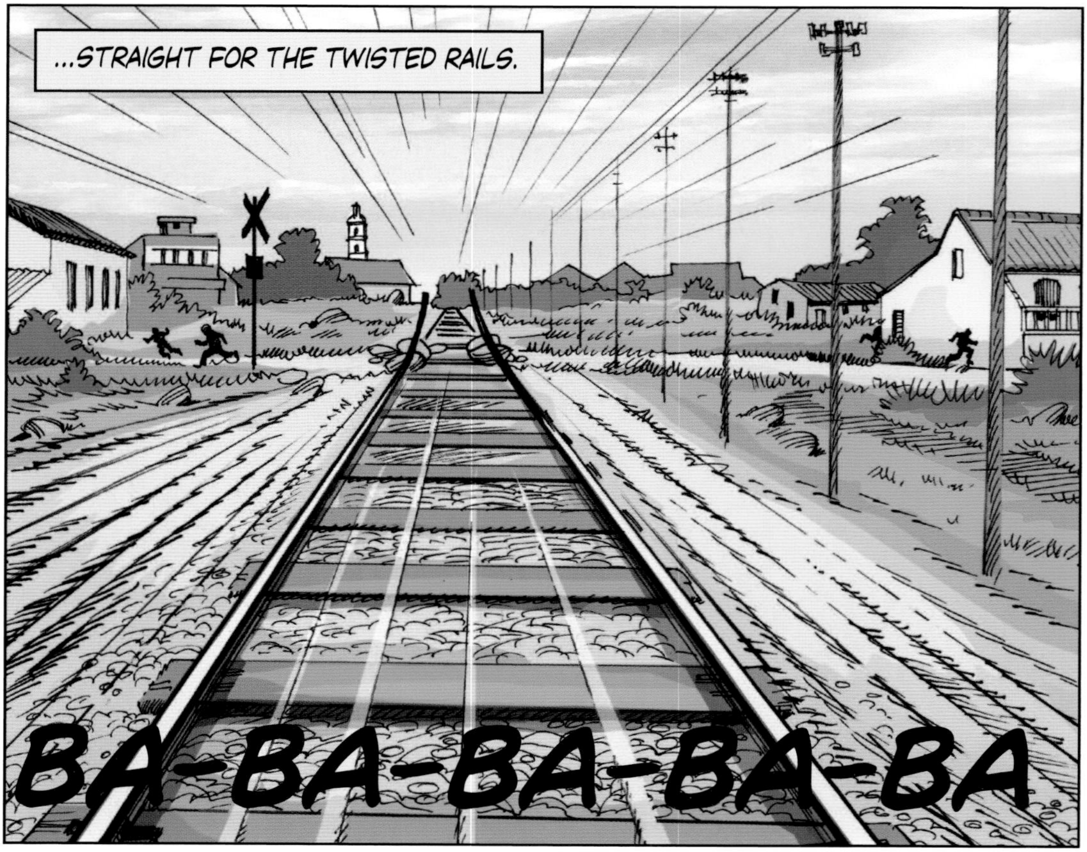
...STRAIGHT FOR THE TWISTED RAILS.
BA-BA-BA-BA-BA

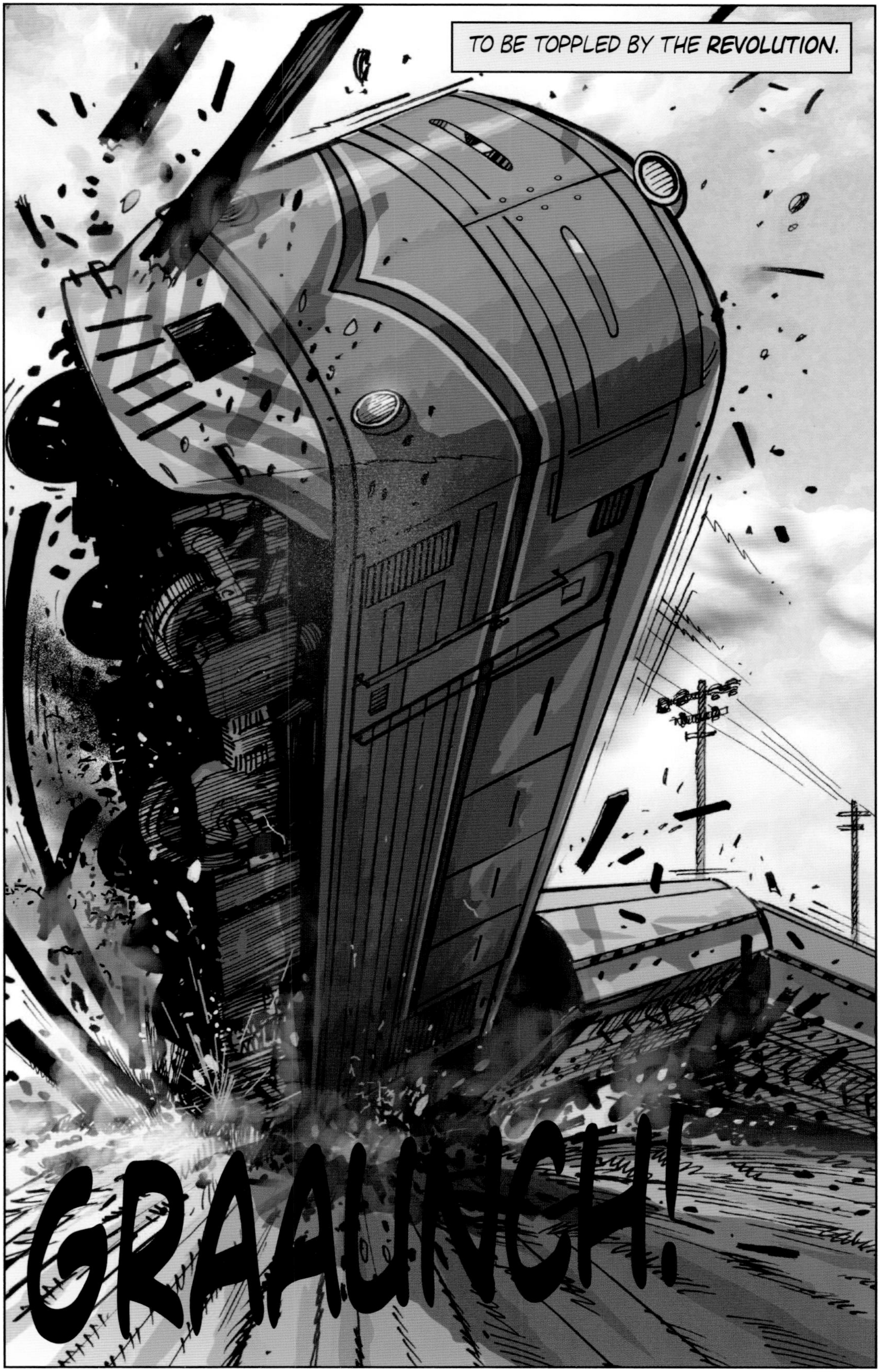
TO BE TOPPLED BY THE REVOLUTION.
GRAAUNCH!

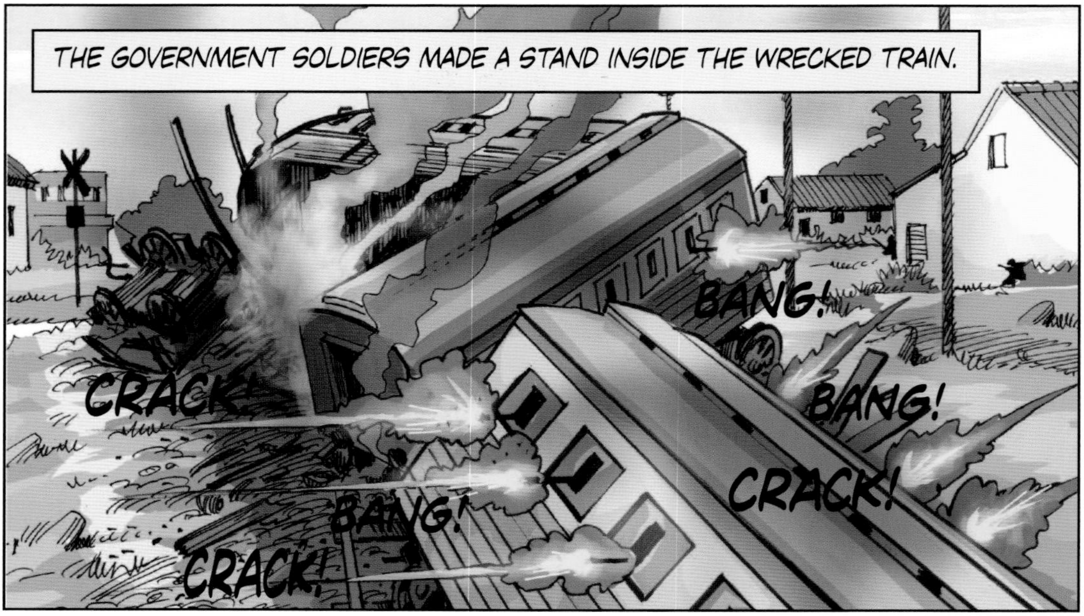
THE GOVERNMENT SOLDIERS MADE A STAND INSIDE THE WRECKED TRAIN.
BANG!
CRACK!
BANG!
CRACK!
BANG!
CRACK!

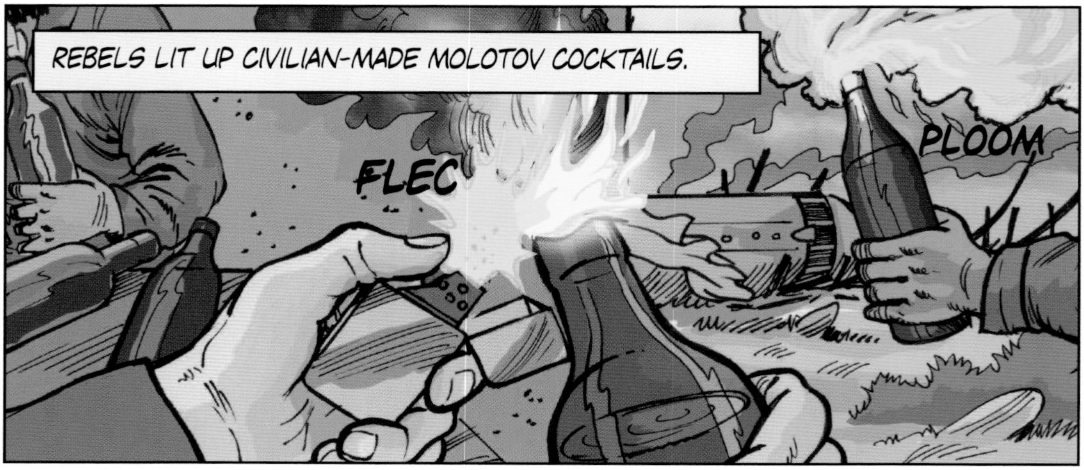
REBELS LIT UP CIVILIAN-MADE MOLOTOV COCKTAILS.
FLEC
PLOOM

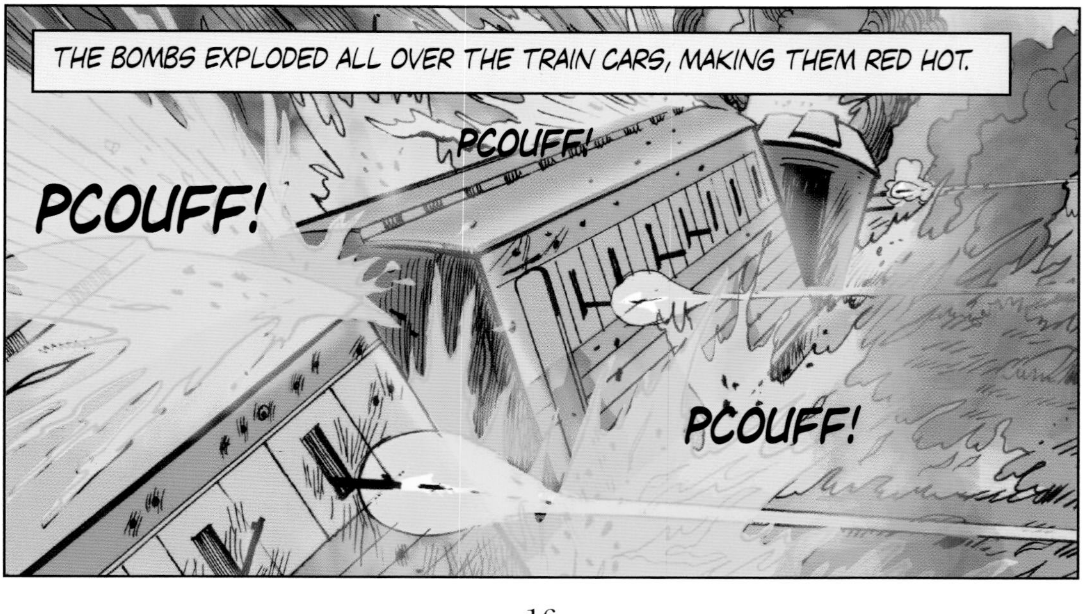
THE BOMBS EXPLODED ALL OVER THE TRAIN CARS, MAKING THEM RED HOT.
PCOUFF!
PCOUFF!
PCOUFF!

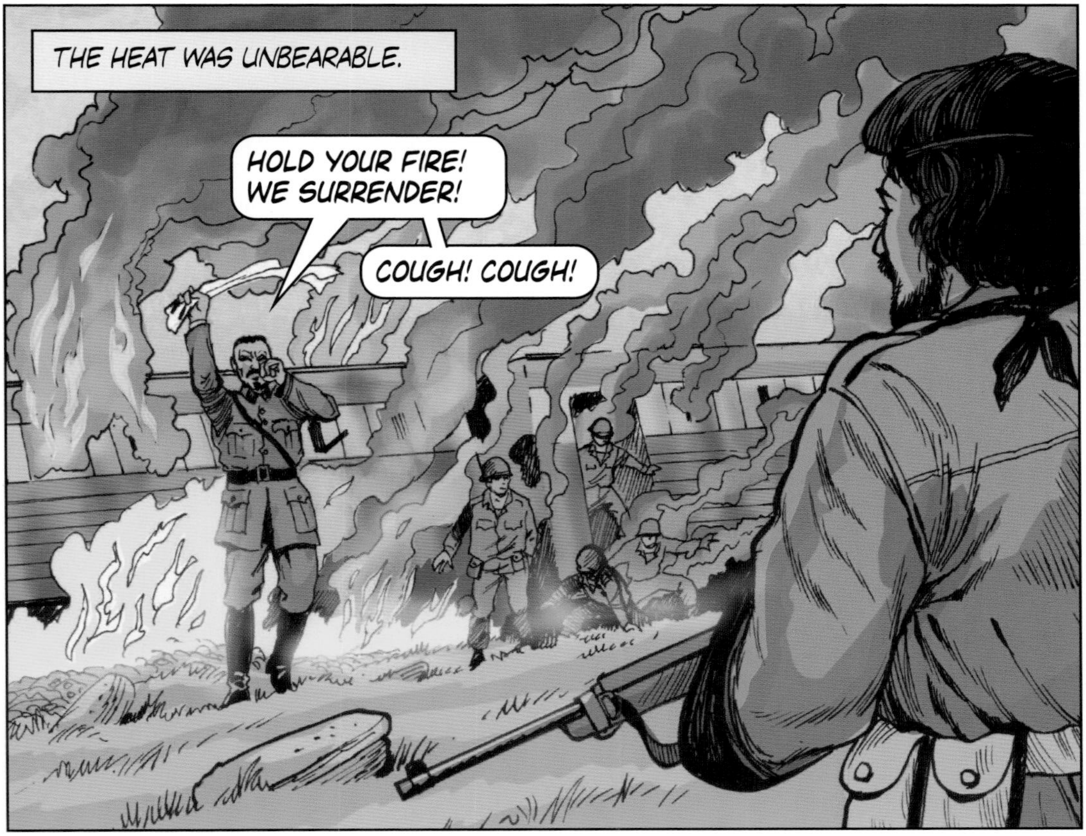
THE HEAT WAS UNBEARABLE.
HOLD YOUR FIRE! WE SURRENDER!
COUGH! COUGH!

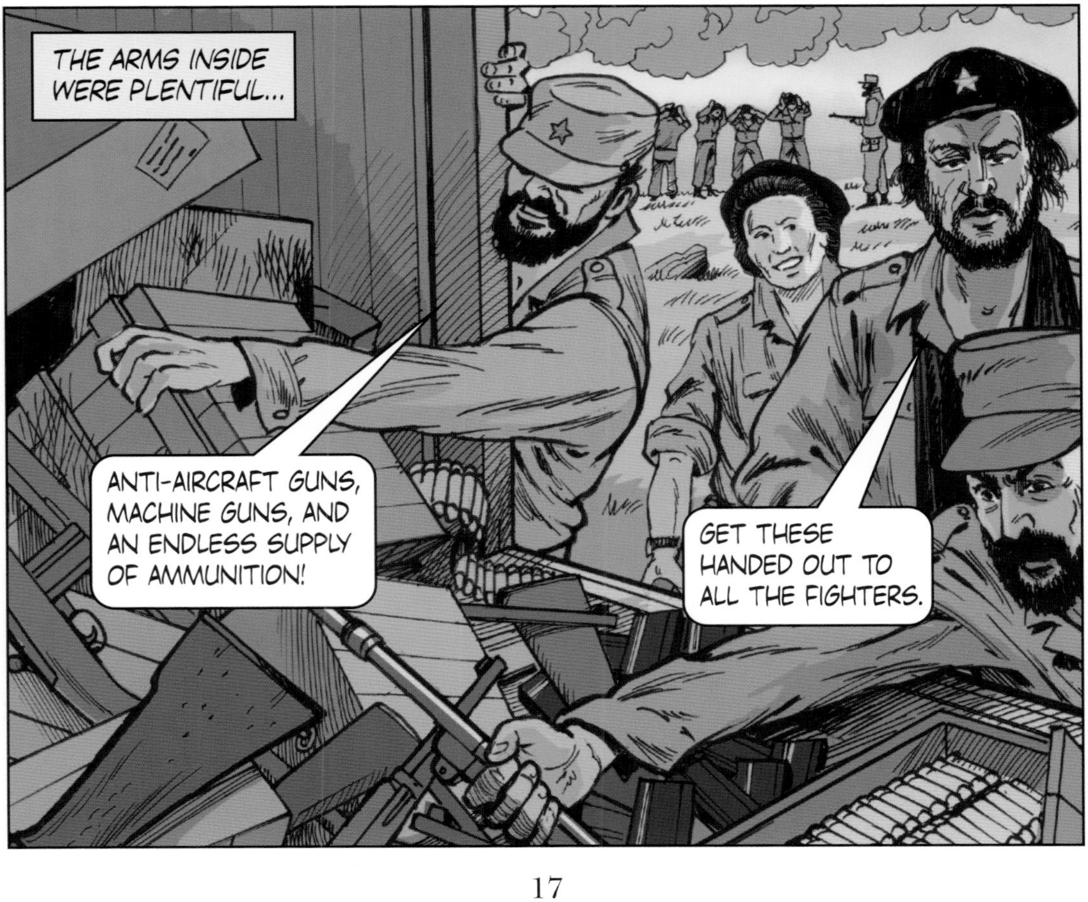
THE ARMS INSIDE WERE PLENTIFUL...
ANTI-AIRCRAFT GUNS, MACHINE GUNS, AND AN ENDLESS SUPPLY OF AMMUNITION!
GET THESE HANDED OUT TO ALL THE FIGHTERS.

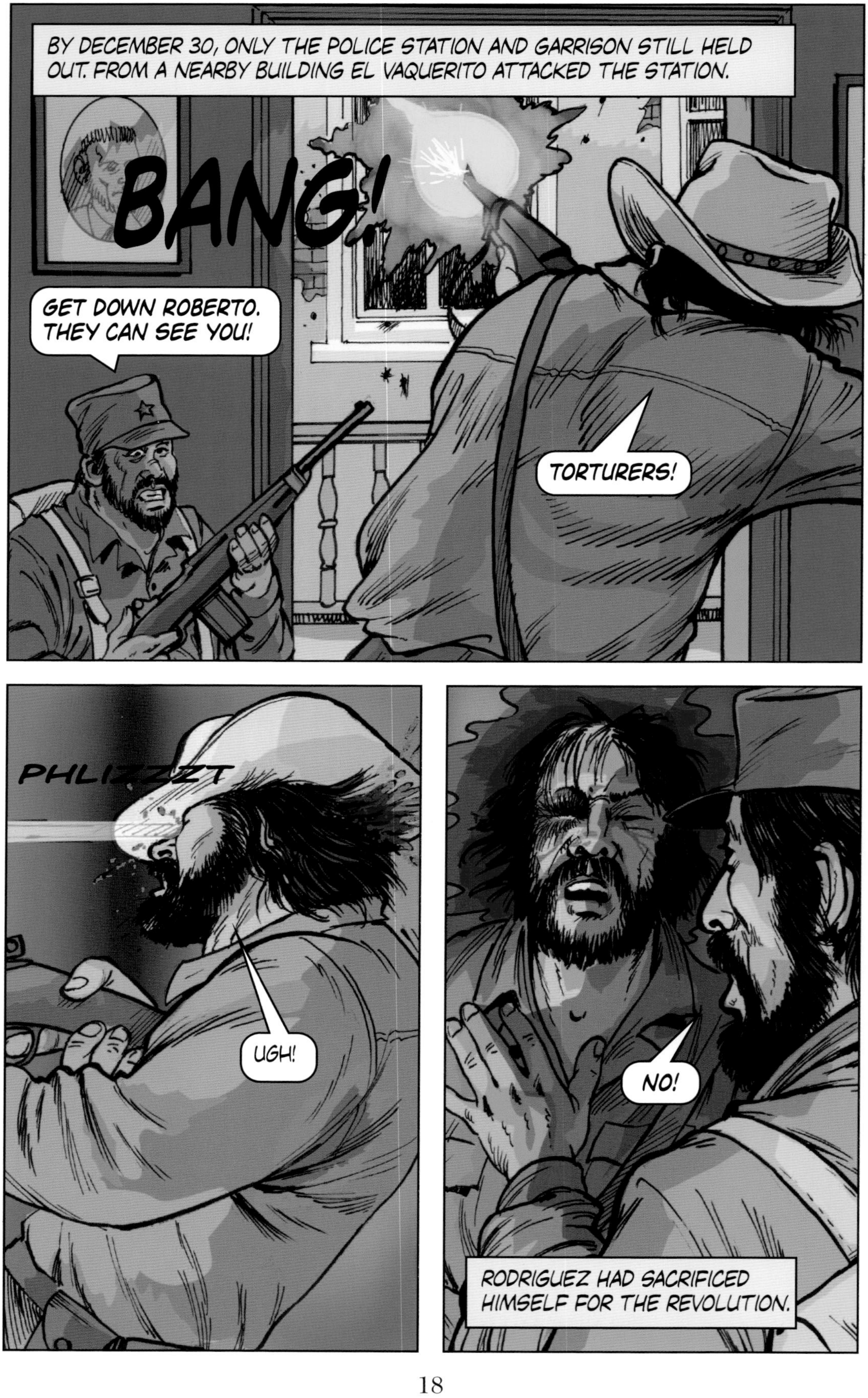
BY DECEMBER 30, ONLY THE POLICE STATION AND GARRISON STILL HELD OUT. FROM A NEARBY BUILDING EL VAQUERITO ATTACKED THE STATION.
BANG!
GET DOWN ROBERTO. THEY CAN SEE YOU!
TORTURERS!
PHLIZZZT
UGH!
NO!
RODRIGUEZ HAD SACRIFICED HIMSELF FOR THE REVOLUTION.

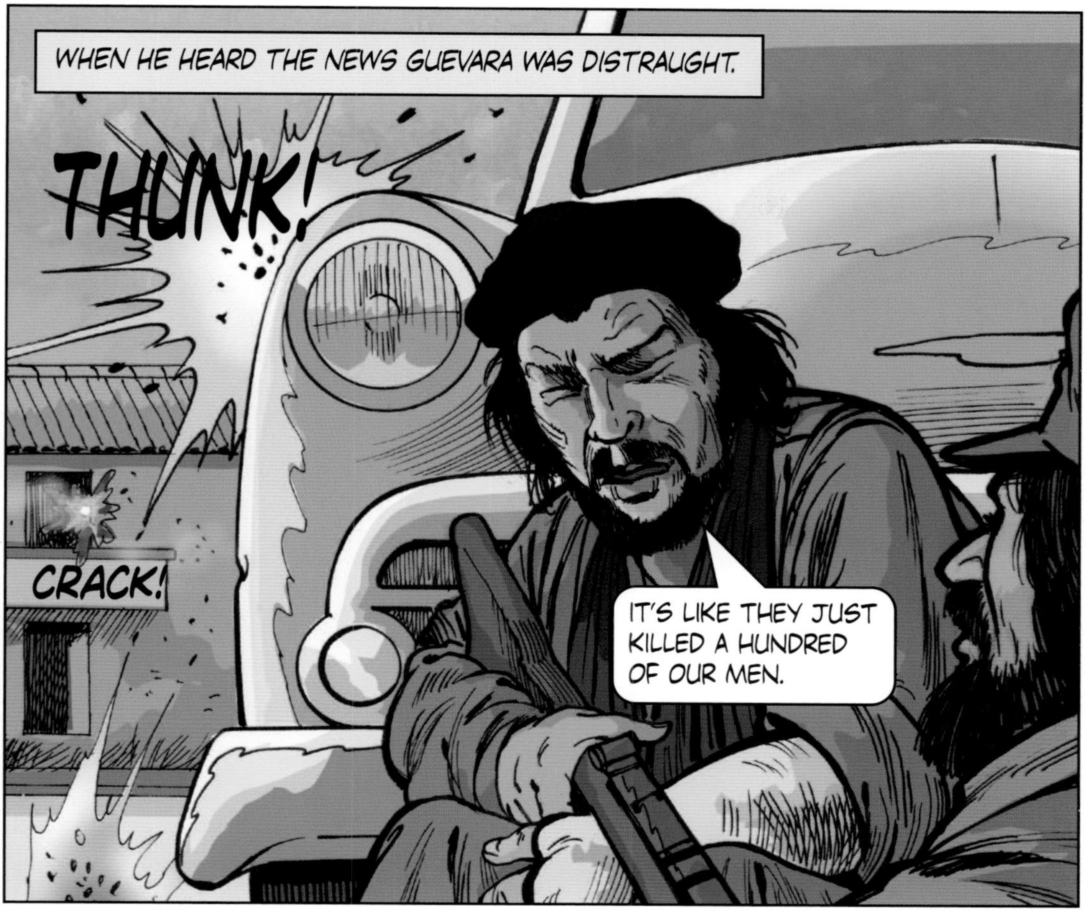
WHEN HE HEARD THE NEWS GUEVARA WAS DISTRAUGHT.
THUNK!
CRACK!
IT'S LIKE THEY JUST KILLED A HUNDRED OF OUR MEN.

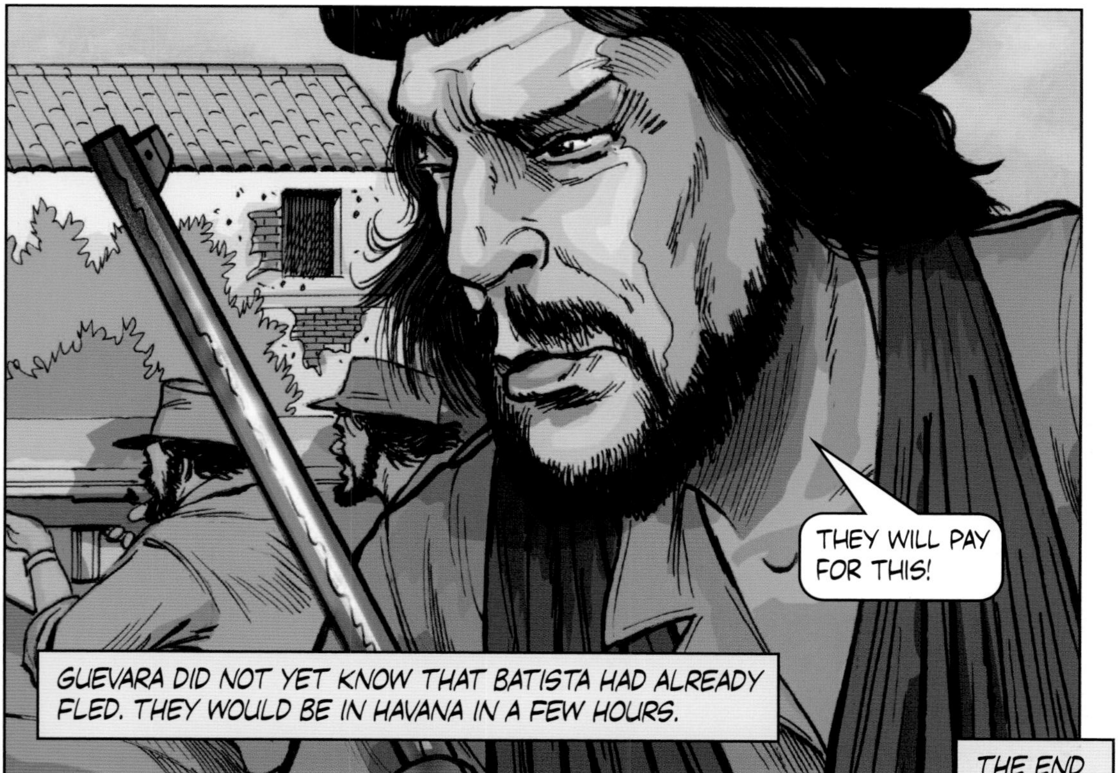
THEY WILL PAY FOR THIS!
GUEVARA DID NOT YET KNOW THAT BATISTA HAD ALREADY FLED. THEY WOULD BE IN HAVANA IN A FEW HOURS.
THE END

THE BAY OF PIGS INVASION, 1961

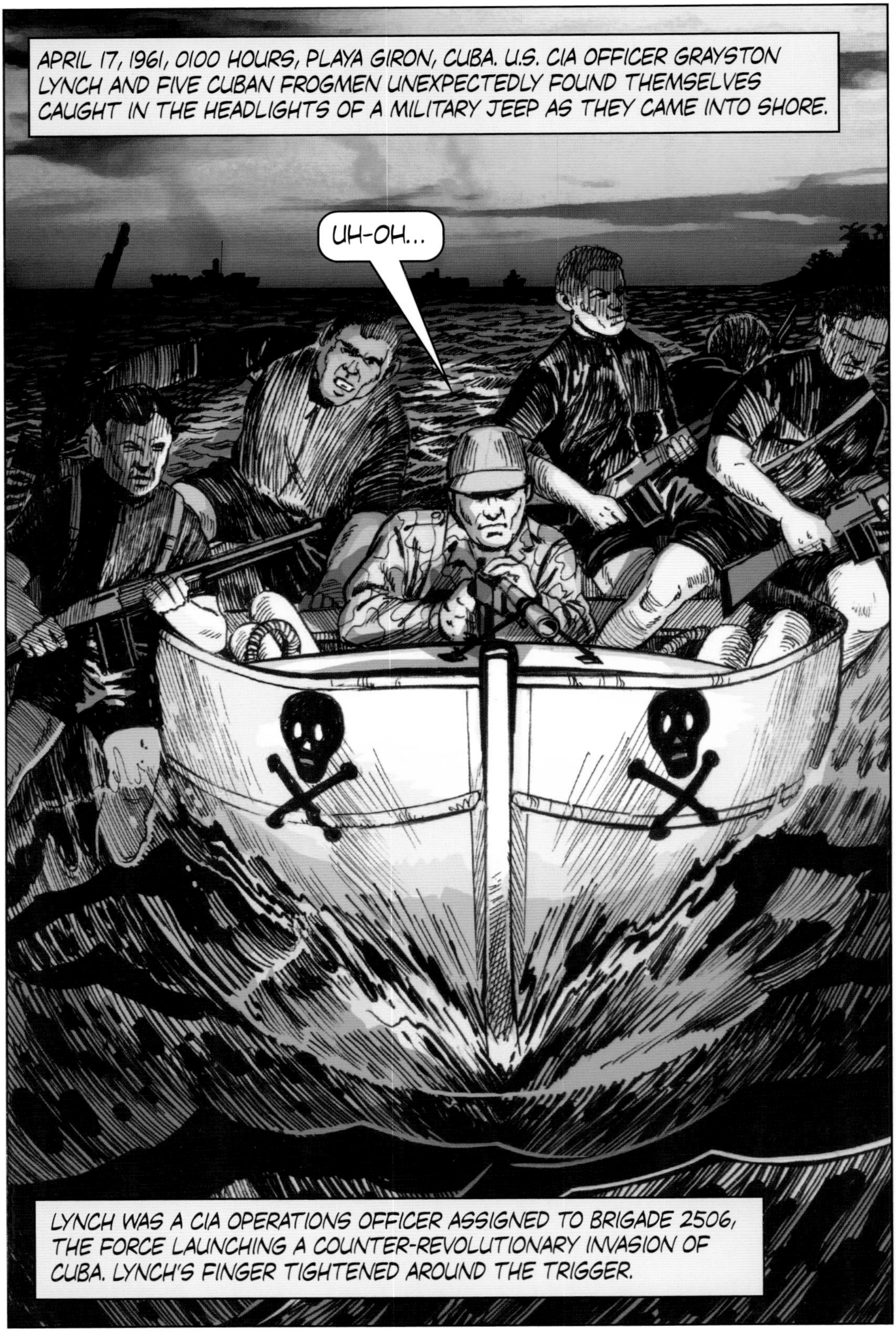
APRIL 17, 1961, 0100 HOURS, PLAYA GIRON, CUBA. U.S. CIA OFFICER GRAYSTON LYNCH AND FIVE CUBAN FROGMEN UNEXPECTEDLY FOUND THEMSELVES CAUGHT IN THE HEADLIGHTS OF A MILITARY JEEP AS THEY CAME INTO SHORE.
UH-OH...
LYNCH WAS A CIA OPERATIONS OFFICER ASSIGNED TO BRIGADE 2506, THE FORCE LAUNCHING A COUNTER-REVOLUTIONARY INVASION OF CUBA. LYNCH'S FINGER TIGHTENED AROUND THE TRIGGER.

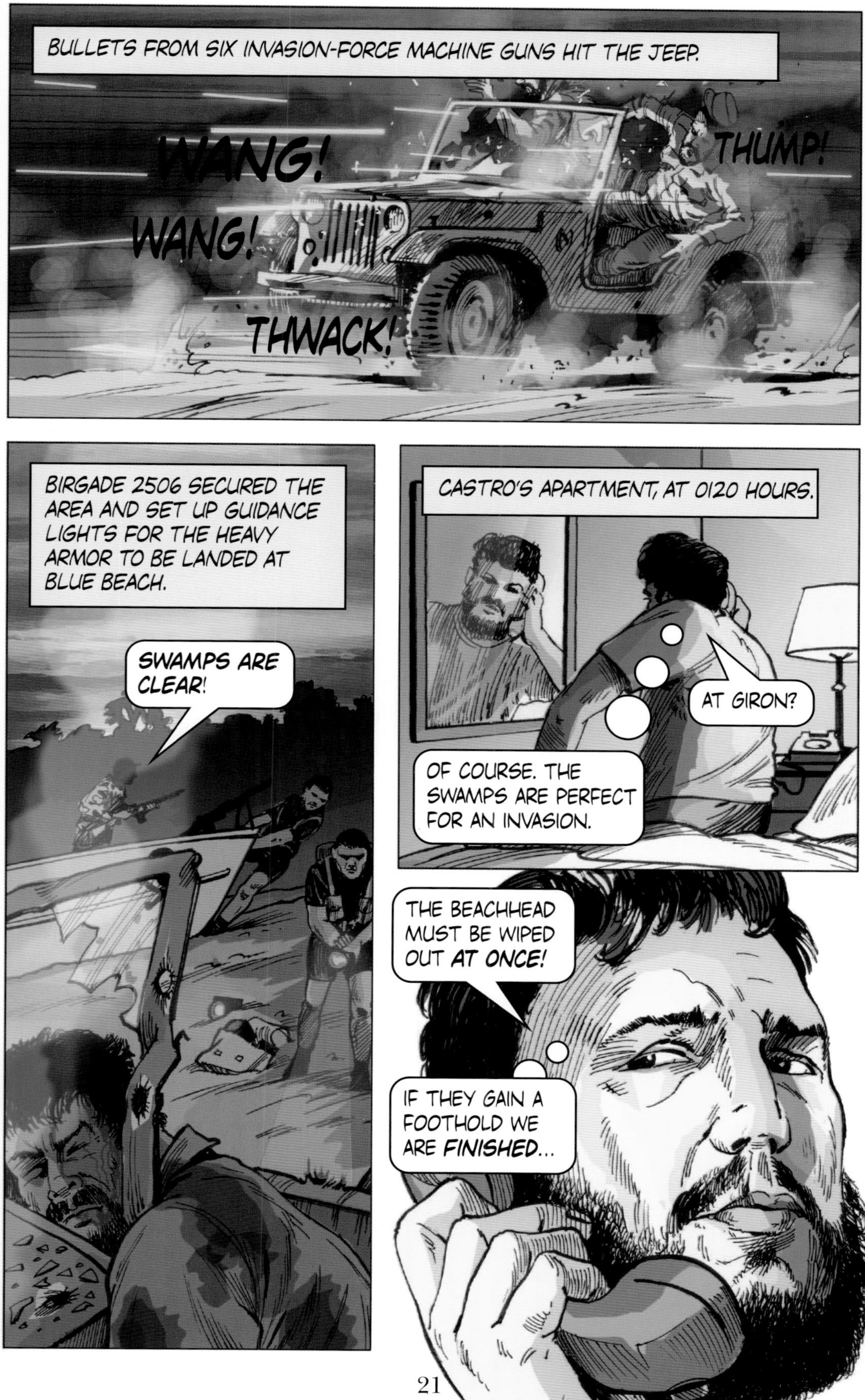
BULLETS FROM SIX INVASION-FORCE MACHINE GUNS HIT THE JEEP.
WANG!
WANG!
THUMP!
THWACK!
BIRGADE 2506 SECURED THE AREA AND SET UP GUIDANCE LIGHTS FOR THE HEAVY ARMOR TO BE LANDED AT BLUE BEACH.
SWAMPS ARE CLEAR!
CASTRO'S APARTMENT, AT 0120 HOURS.
AT GIRON?
OF COURSE. THE SWAMPS ARE PERFECT FOR AN INVASION.
THE BEACHHEAD MUST BE WIPED OUT AT ONCE!
IF THEY GAIN A FOOTHOLD WE ARE FINISHED...

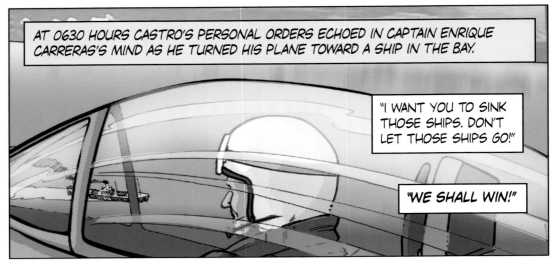

AT 0630 HOURS CASTRO'S PERSONAL ORDERS ECHOED IN CAPTAIN ENRIQUE CARRERAS'S MIND AS HE TURNED HIS PLANE TOWARD A SHIP IN THE BAY.

"I WANT YOU TO SINK THOSE SHIPS. DON'T LET THOSE SHIPS GO!"

"WE SHALL WIN!"

THE HOUSTON WAS CARRYING THE FIFTH BRIGADE - 450 MEN.

ALSO ONBOARD WAS THE MISSION'S RADIO TRUCK.

CARRERAS FIRED ALL EIGHT ROCKETS...

SCREEE!

...STRIKING THE HOUSTON AMIDSHIPS.

KRUMP!

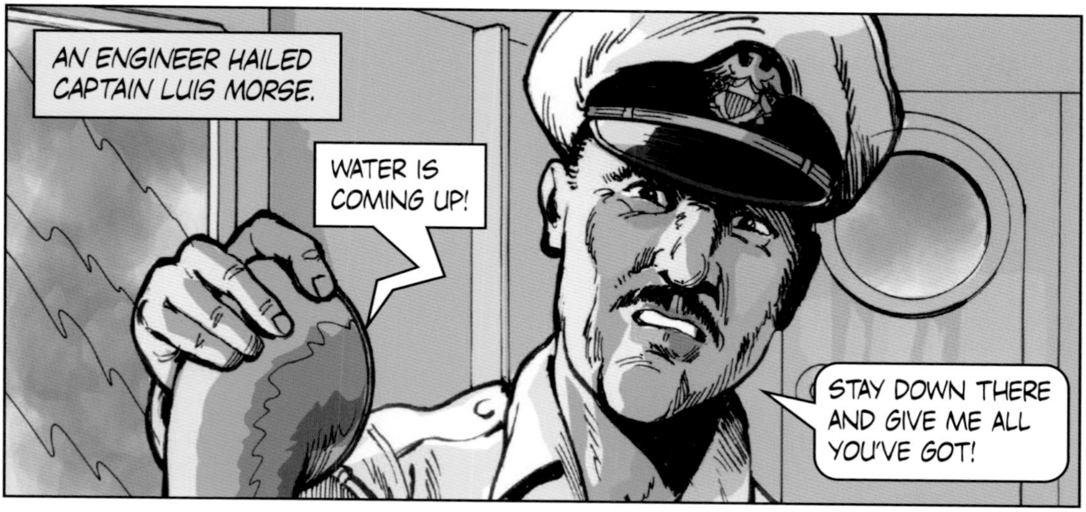
AN ENGINEER HAILED CAPTAIN LUIS MORSE.
WATER IS COMING UP!
STAY DOWN THERE AND GIVE ME ALL YOU'VE GOT!

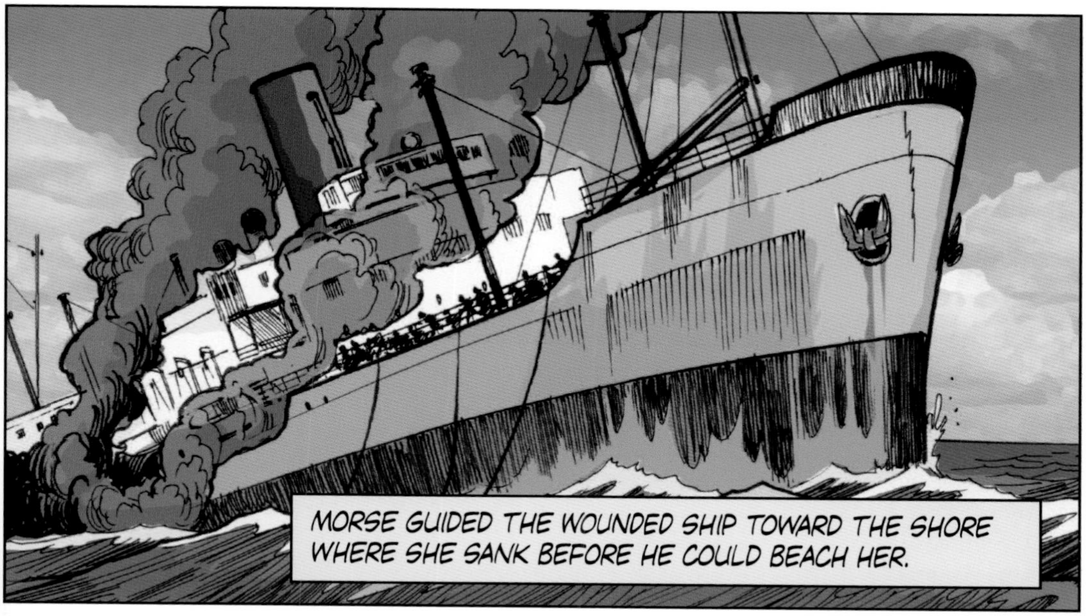
MORSE GUIDED THE WOUNDED SHIP TOWARD THE SHORE WHERE SHE SANK BEFORE HE COULD BEACH HER.

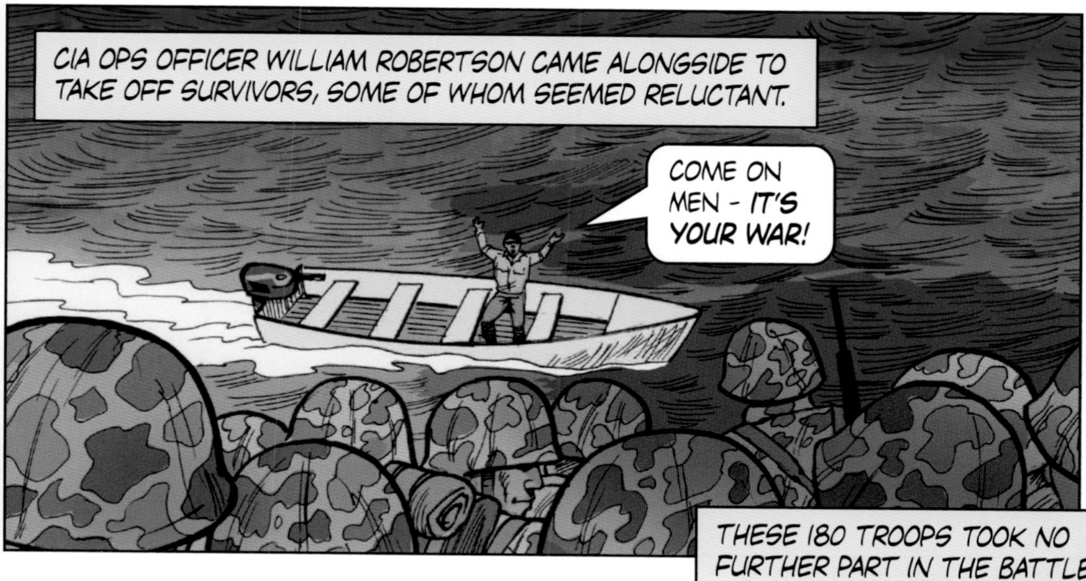
CIA OPS OFFICER WILLIAM ROBERTSON CAME ALONGSIDE TO TAKE OFF SURVIVORS, SOME OF WHOM SEEMED RELUCTANT.
COME ON MEN - IT'S YOUR WAR!
THESE 180 TROOPS TOOK NO FURTHER PART IN THE BATTLE.

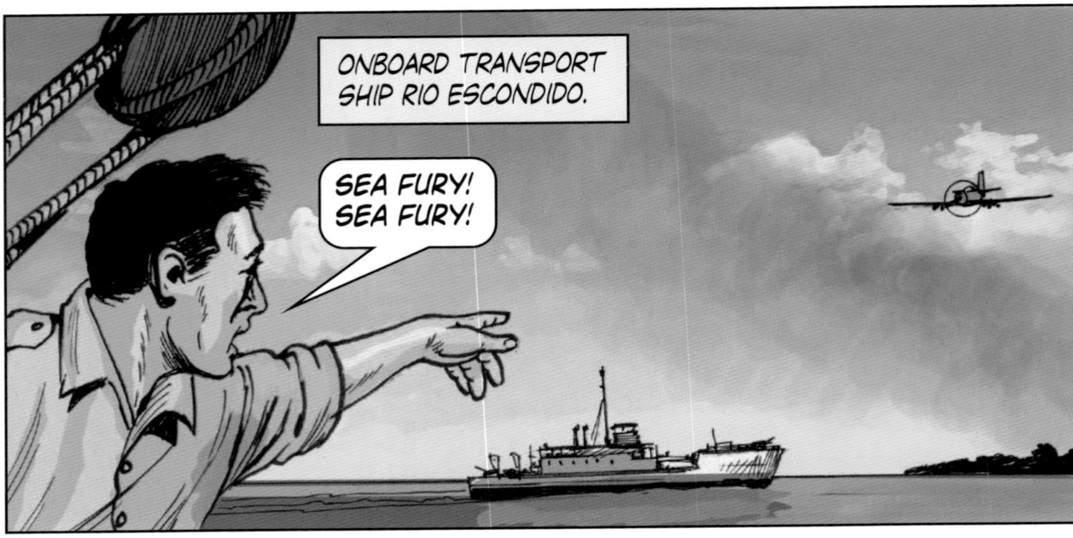
ONBOARD TRANSPORT SHIP RIO ESCONDIDO.
SEA FURY! SEA FURY!

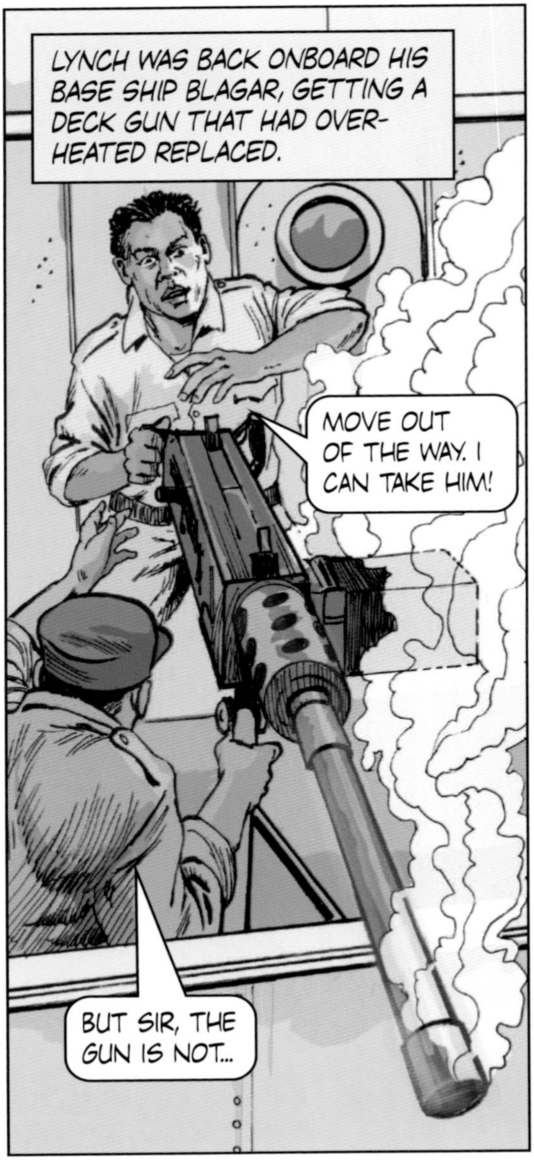
LYNCH WAS BACK ONBOARD HIS BASE SHIP BLAGAR, GETTING A DECK GUN THAT HAD OVER-HEATED REPLACED.
MOVE OUT OF THE WAY. I CAN TAKE HIM!
BUT SIR, THE GUN IS NOT...

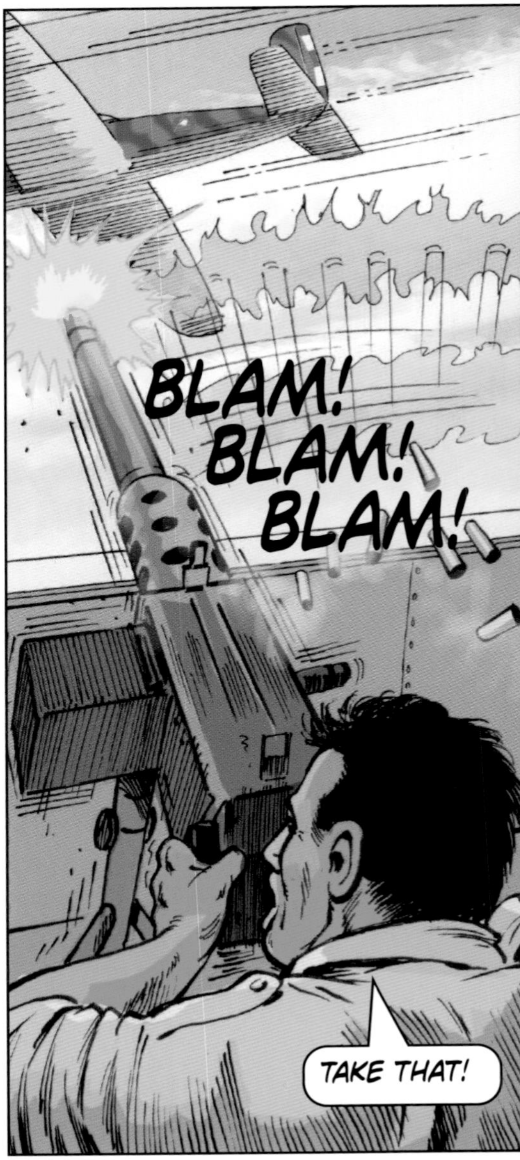
BLAM! BLAM! BLAM!
TAKE THAT!

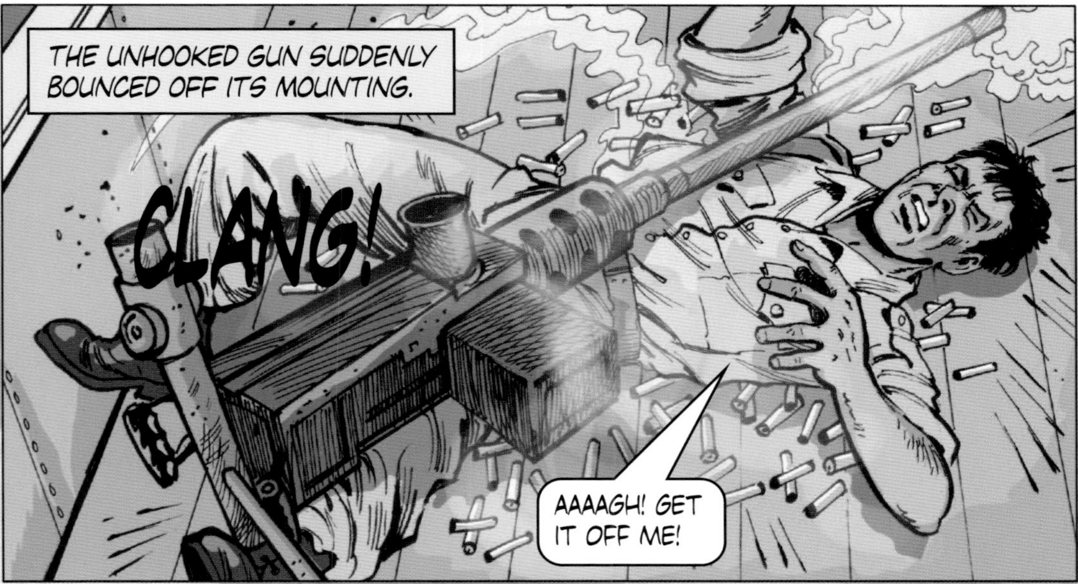
THE UNHOOKED GUN SUDDENLY BOUNCED OFF ITS MOUNTING.
CLANG!
AAAAGH! GET IT OFF ME!

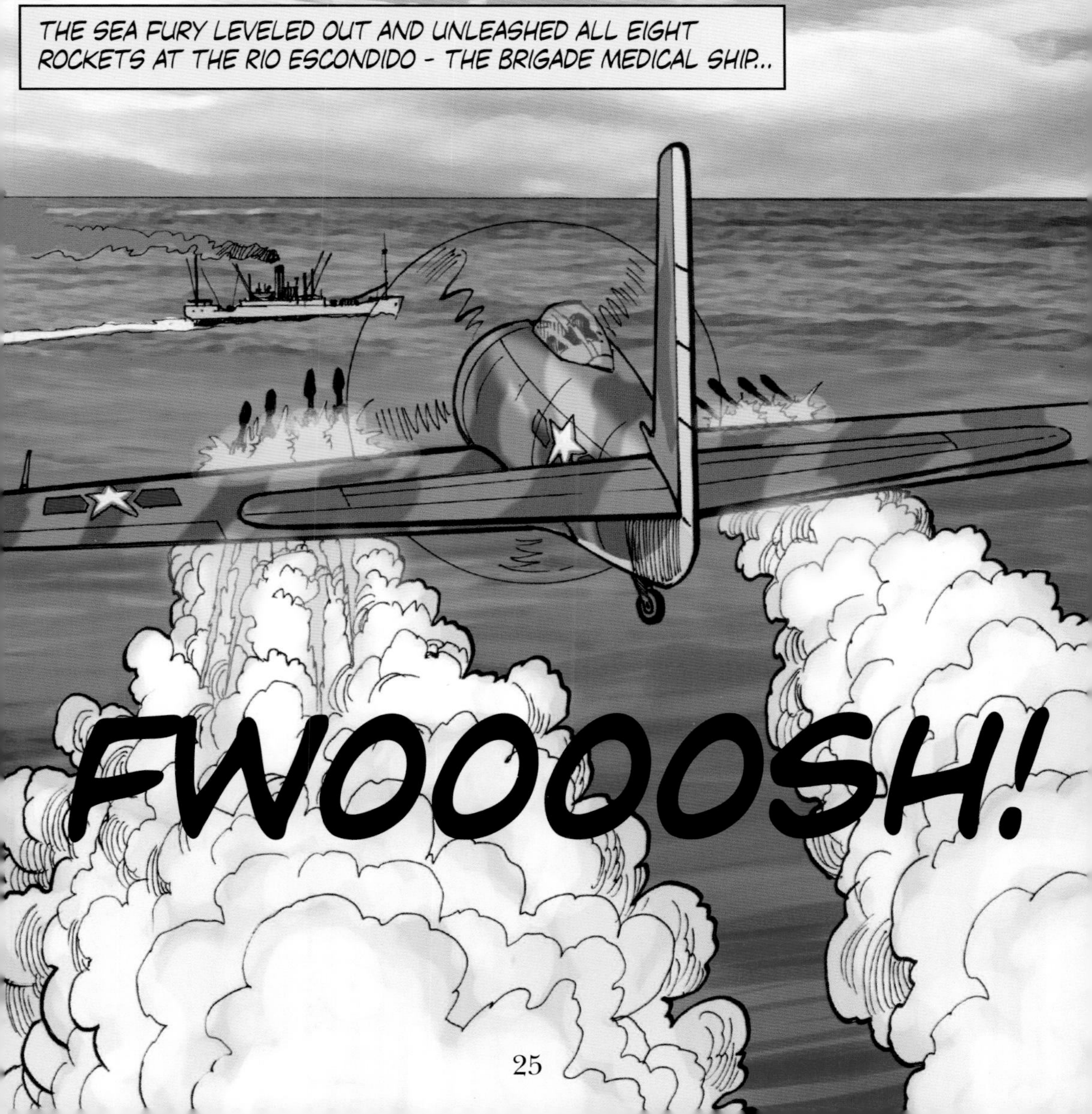
THE SEA FURY LEVELED OUT AND UNLEASHED ALL EIGHT ROCKETS AT THE RIO ESCONDIDO - THE BRIGADE MEDICAL SHIP...
FWOOOOSH!

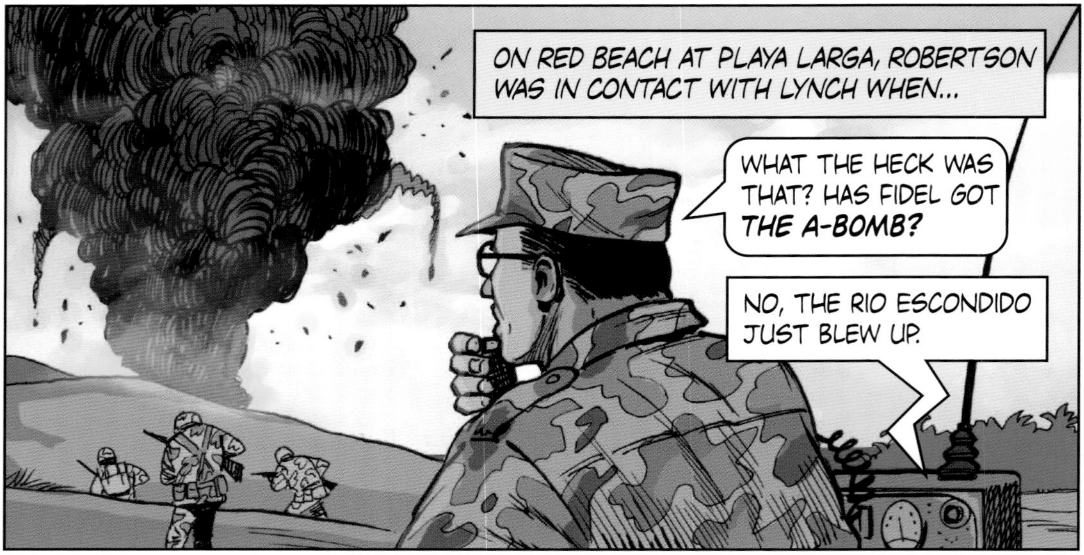
ON RED BEACH AT PLAYA LARGA, ROBERTSON WAS IN CONTACT WITH LYNCH WHEN...
WHAT THE HECK WAS THAT? HAS FIDEL GOT THE A-BOMB?
NO, THE RIO ESCONDIDO JUST BLEW UP.

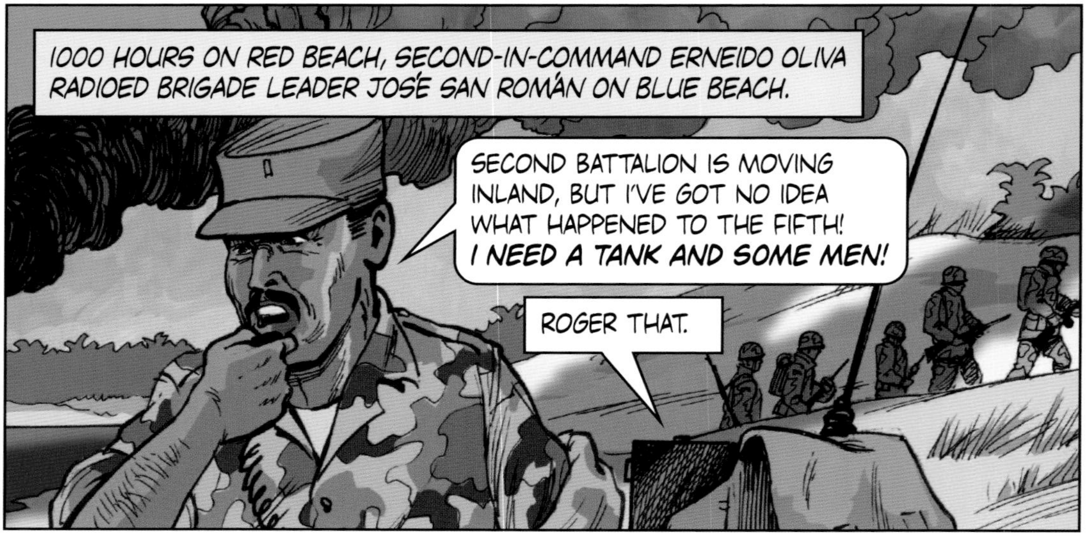
1000 HOURS ON RED BEACH, SECOND-IN-COMMAND ERNEIDO OLIVA RADIOED BRIGADE LEADER JOSÉ SAN ROMÁN ON BLUE BEACH.
SECOND BATTALION IS MOVING INLAND, BUT I'VE GOT NO IDEA WHAT HAPPENED TO THE FIFTH! I NEED A TANK AND SOME MEN!
ROGER THAT.

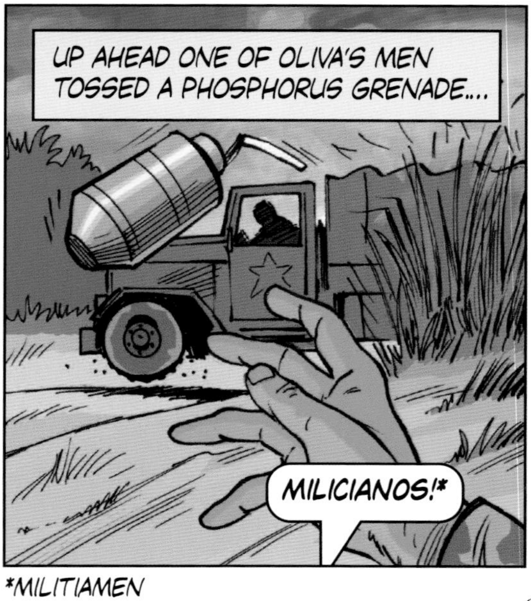
UP AHEAD ONE OF OLIVA'S MEN TOSSED A PHOSPHORUS GRENADE....
MILICIANOS!*

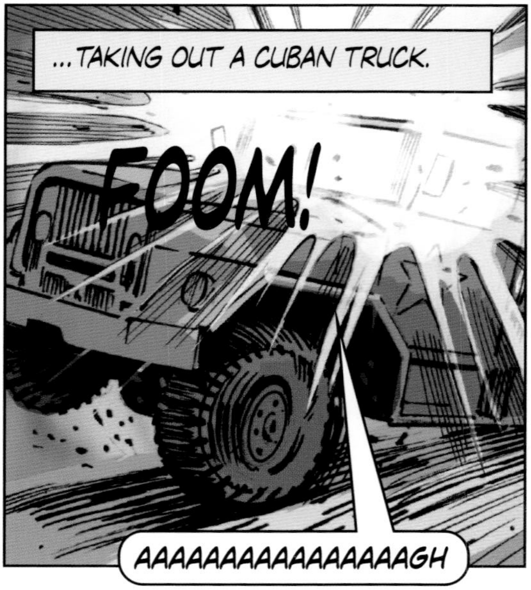
...TAKING OUT A CUBAN TRUCK.
FOOM!
AAAAAAAAAAAAAAAAGH

*MILITIAMEN

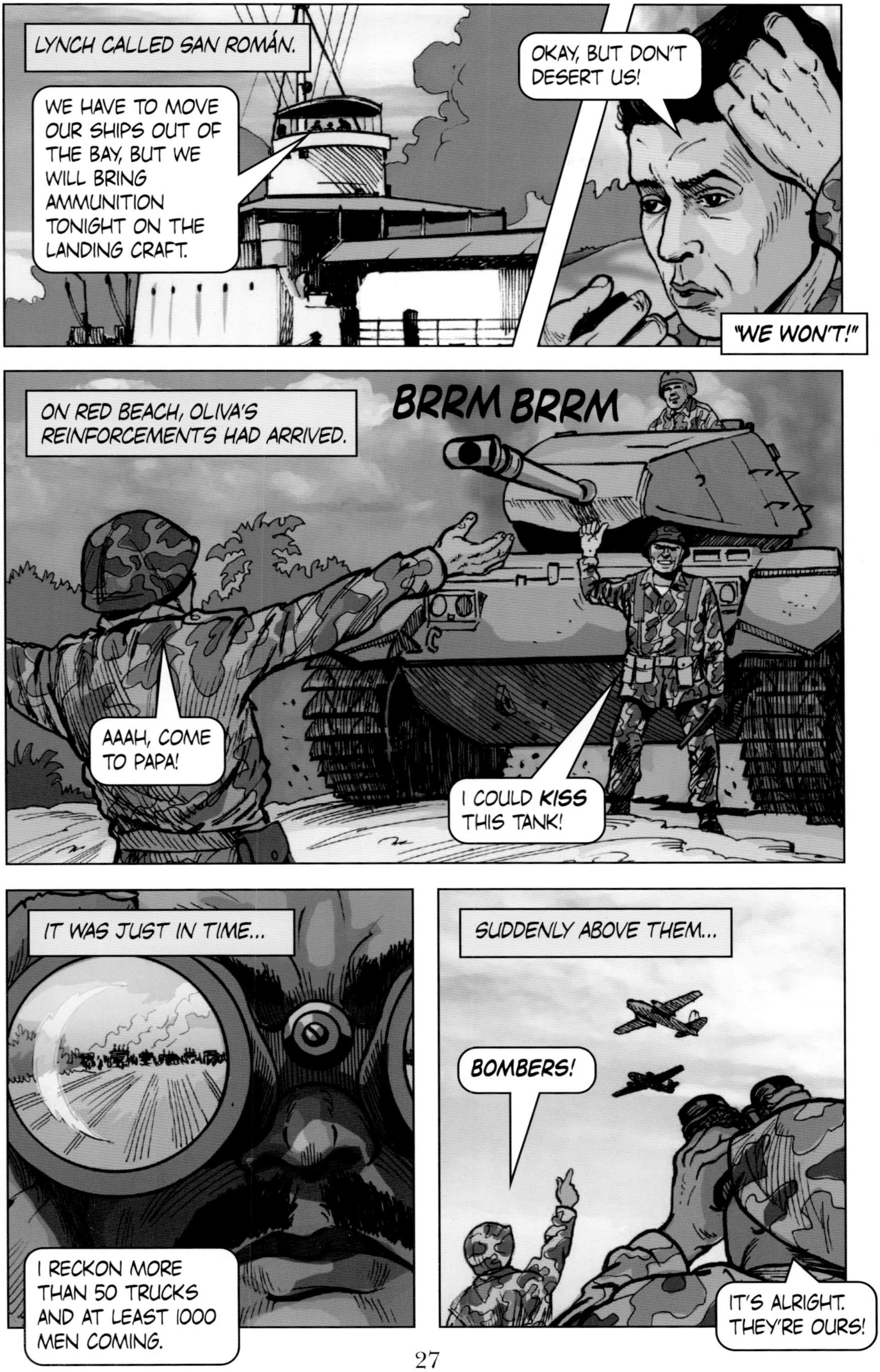
LYNCH CALLED SAN ROMÁN.
WE HAVE TO MOVE OUR SHIPS OUT OF THE BAY, BUT WE WILL BRING AMMUNITION TONIGHT ON THE LANDING CRAFT.
OKAY, BUT DON'T DESERT US!
"WE WON'T!"
ON RED BEACH, OLIVA'S REINFORCEMENTS HAD ARRIVED.
BRRM BRRM
AAAH, COME TO PAPA!
I COULD KISS THIS TANK!
IT WAS JUST IN TIME...
I RECKON MORE THAN 50 TRUCKS AND AT LEAST 1000 MEN COMING.
SUDDENLY ABOVE THEM...
BOMBERS!
IT'S ALRIGHT. THEY'RE OURS!

OLIVA RADIOED THE PILOT, JOSE CRESPO.

THE COLUMN ON THE ROAD IS ENEMY. **ATTACK THEM NOW!**

WILL DO!

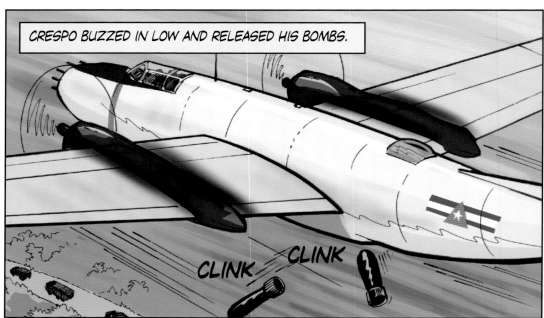

CRESPO BUZZED IN LOW AND RELEASED HIS BOMBS.

CLINK   CLINK

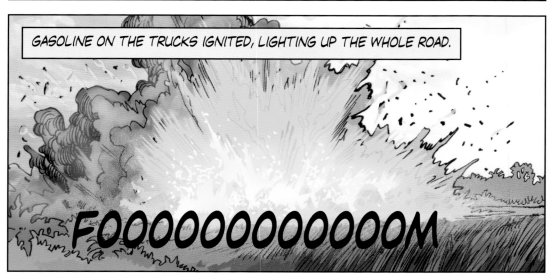

GASOLINE ON THE TRUCKS IGNITED, LIGHTING UP THE WHOLE ROAD.

FOOOOOOOOOOOOOM

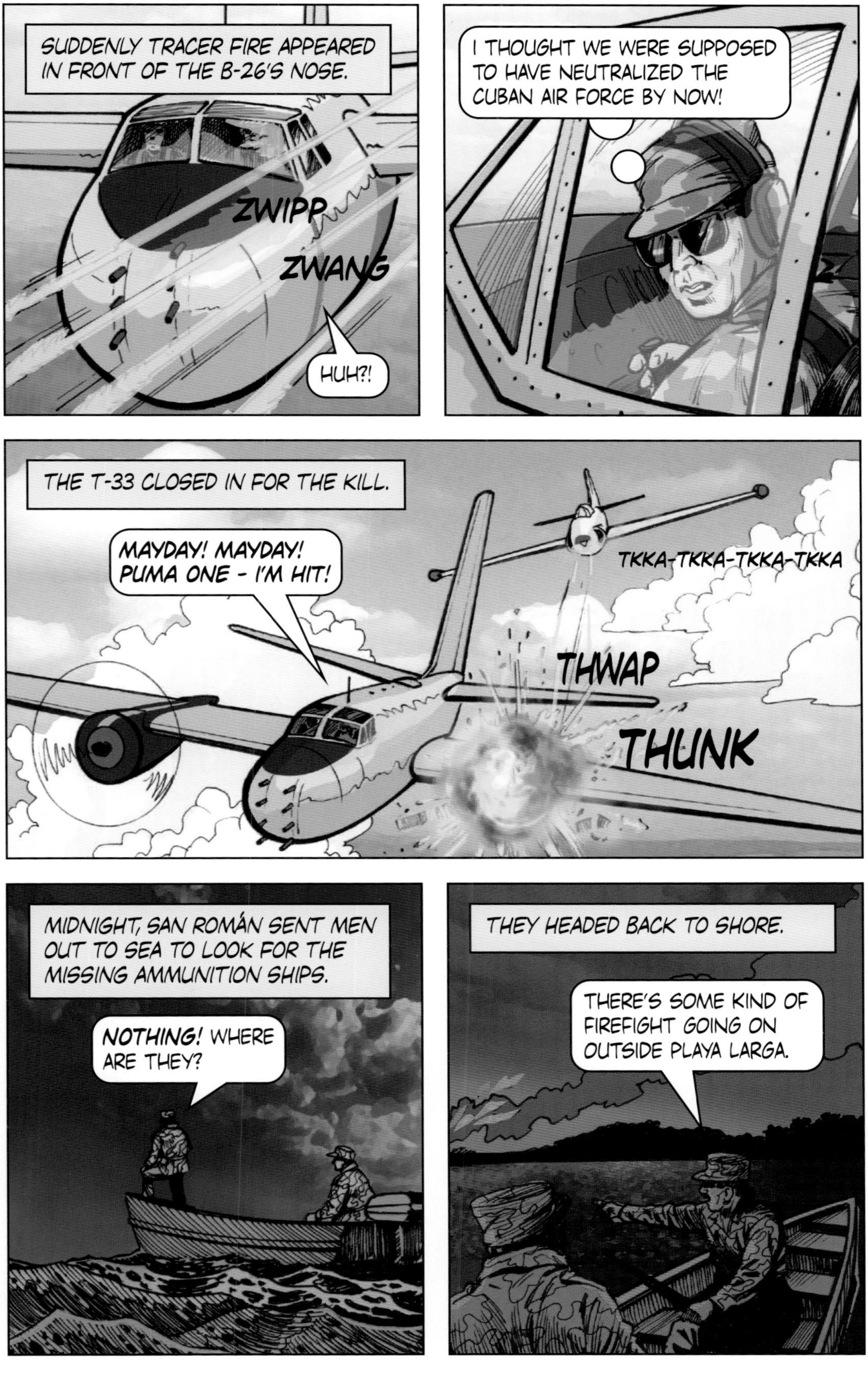
SUDDENLY TRACER FIRE APPEARED IN FRONT OF THE B-26'S NOSE.
ZWIPP
ZWANG
HUH?!
I THOUGHT WE WERE SUPPOSED TO HAVE NEUTRALIZED THE CUBAN AIR FORCE BY NOW!
THE T-33 CLOSED IN FOR THE KILL.
MAYDAY! MAYDAY! PUMA ONE - I'M HIT!
TKKA-TKKA-TKKA-TKKA
THWAP
THUNK
MIDNIGHT, SAN ROMÁN SENT MEN OUT TO SEA TO LOOK FOR THE MISSING AMMUNITION SHIPS.
NOTHING! WHERE ARE THEY?
THEY HEADED BACK TO SHORE.
THERE'S SOME KIND OF FIREFIGHT GOING ON OUTSIDE PLAYA LARGA.

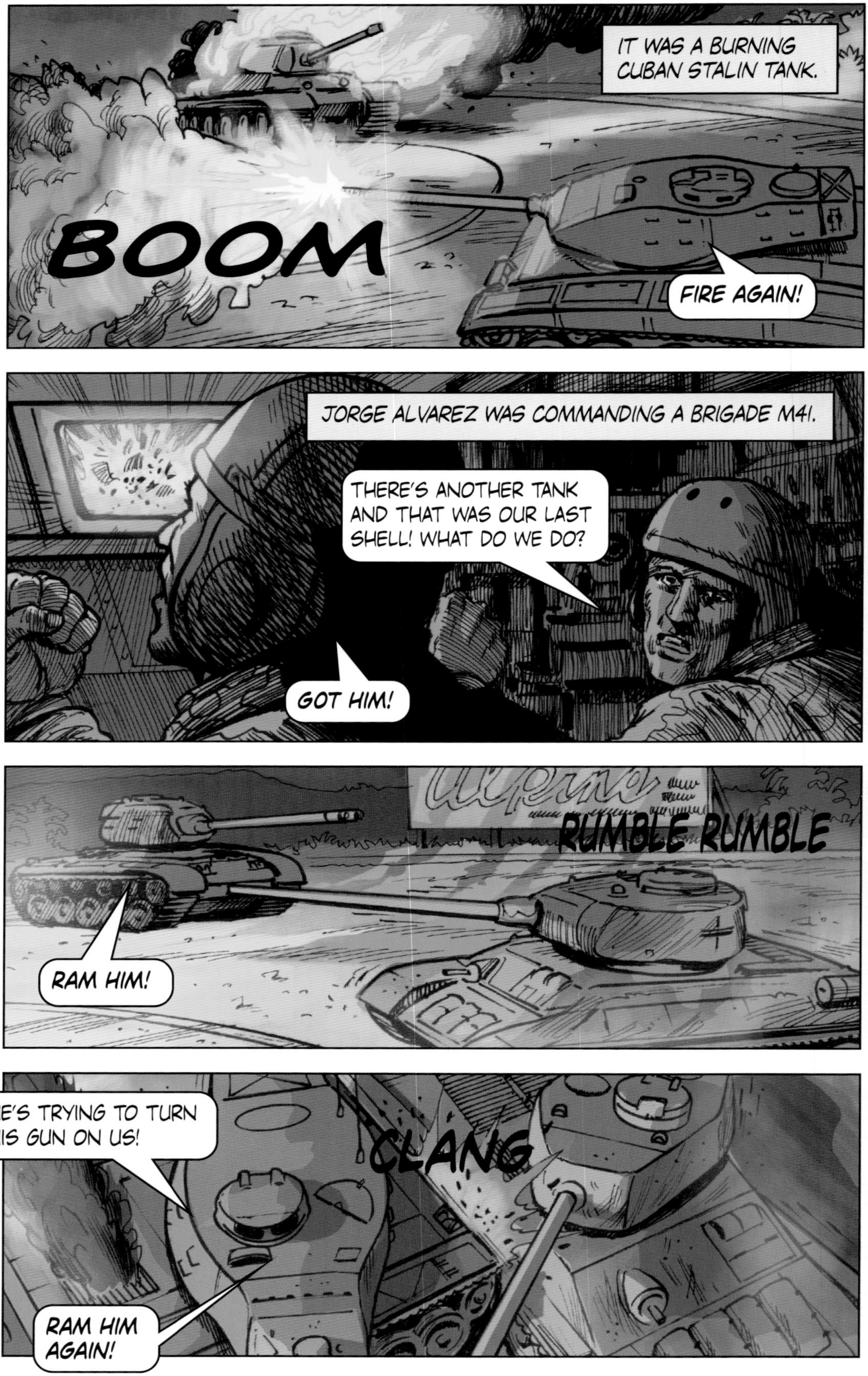
IT WAS A BURNING CUBAN STALIN TANK.
BOOM
FIRE AGAIN!
JORGE ALVAREZ WAS COMMANDING A BRIGADE M41.
GOT HIM!
THERE'S ANOTHER TANK AND THAT WAS OUR LAST SHELL! WHAT DO WE DO?
RUMBLE RUMBLE
RAM HIM!
HE'S TRYING TO TURN HIS GUN ON US!
CLANG
RAM HIM AGAIN!

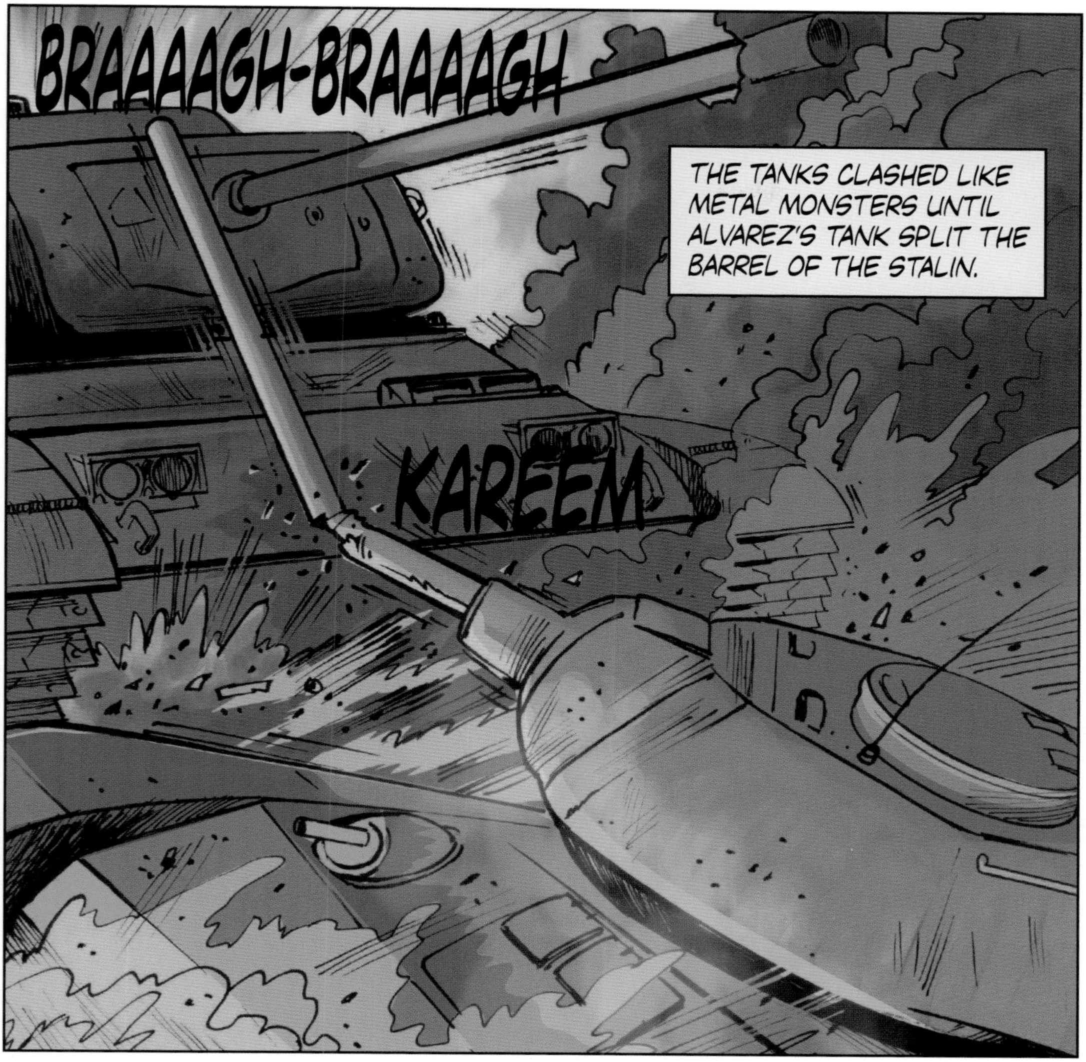
BRAAAAGH-BRAAAAGH
THE TANKS CLASHED LIKE METAL MONSTERS UNTIL ALVAREZ'S TANK SPLIT THE BARREL OF THE STALIN.
KAREEM

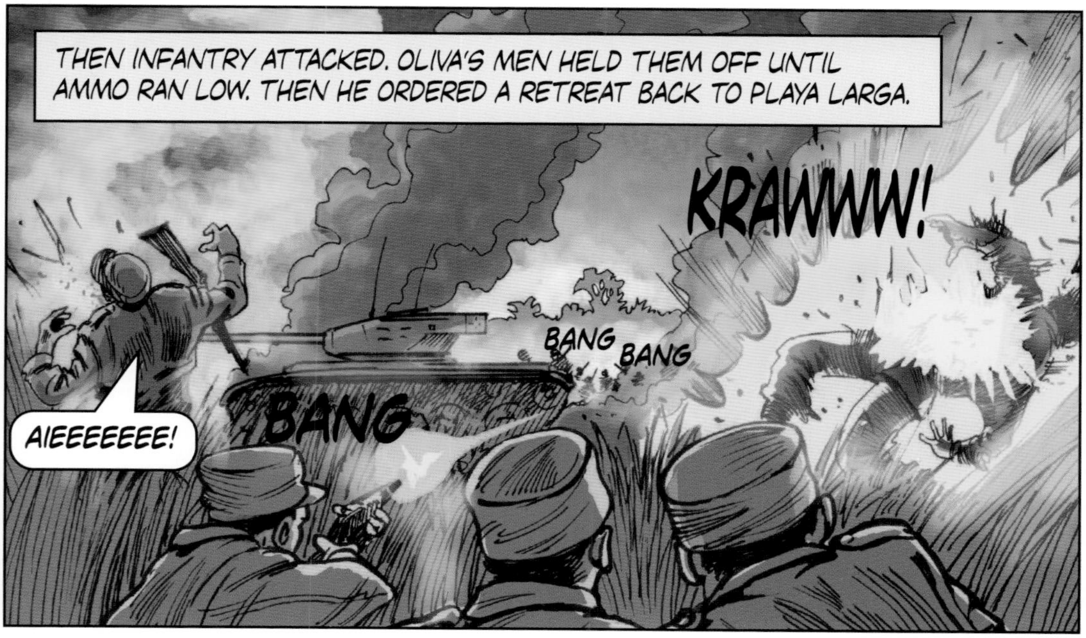
THEN INFANTRY ATTACKED. OLIVA'S MEN HELD THEM OFF UNTIL AMMO RAN LOW. THEN HE ORDERED A RETREAT BACK TO PLAYA LARGA.
KRAWWW!
AIEEEEEEE!
BANG
BANG
BANG

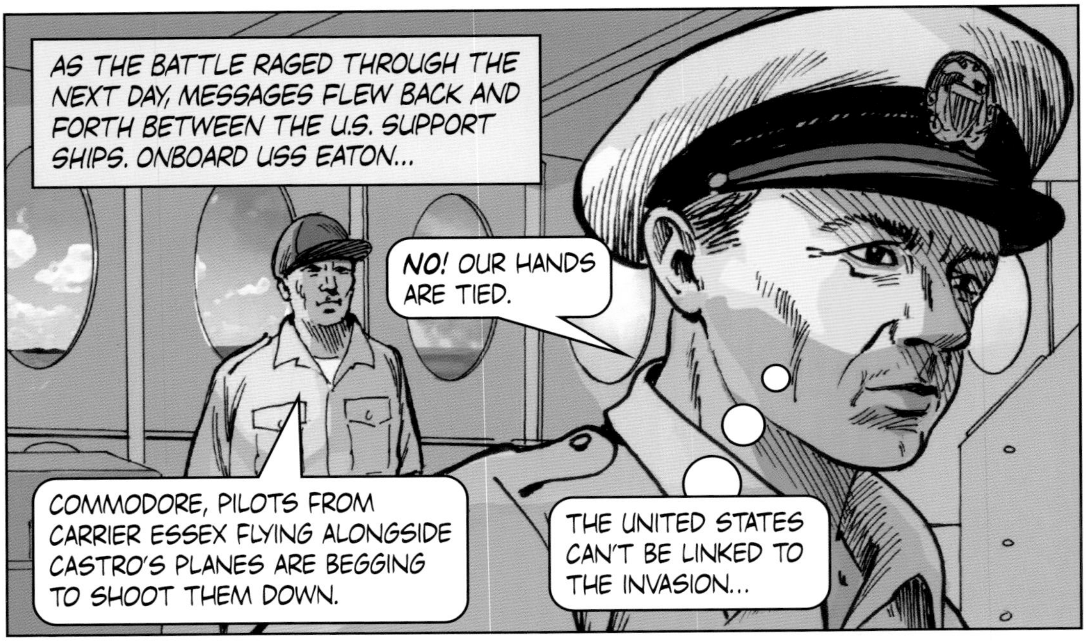
AS THE BATTLE RAGED THROUGH THE NEXT DAY, MESSAGES FLEW BACK AND FORTH BETWEEN THE U.S. SUPPORT SHIPS. ONBOARD USS EATON...
COMMODORE, PILOTS FROM CARRIER ESSEX FLYING ALONGSIDE CASTRO'S PLANES ARE BEGGING TO SHOOT THEM DOWN.
NO! OUR HANDS ARE TIED.
THE UNITED STATES CAN'T BE LINKED TO THE INVASION...

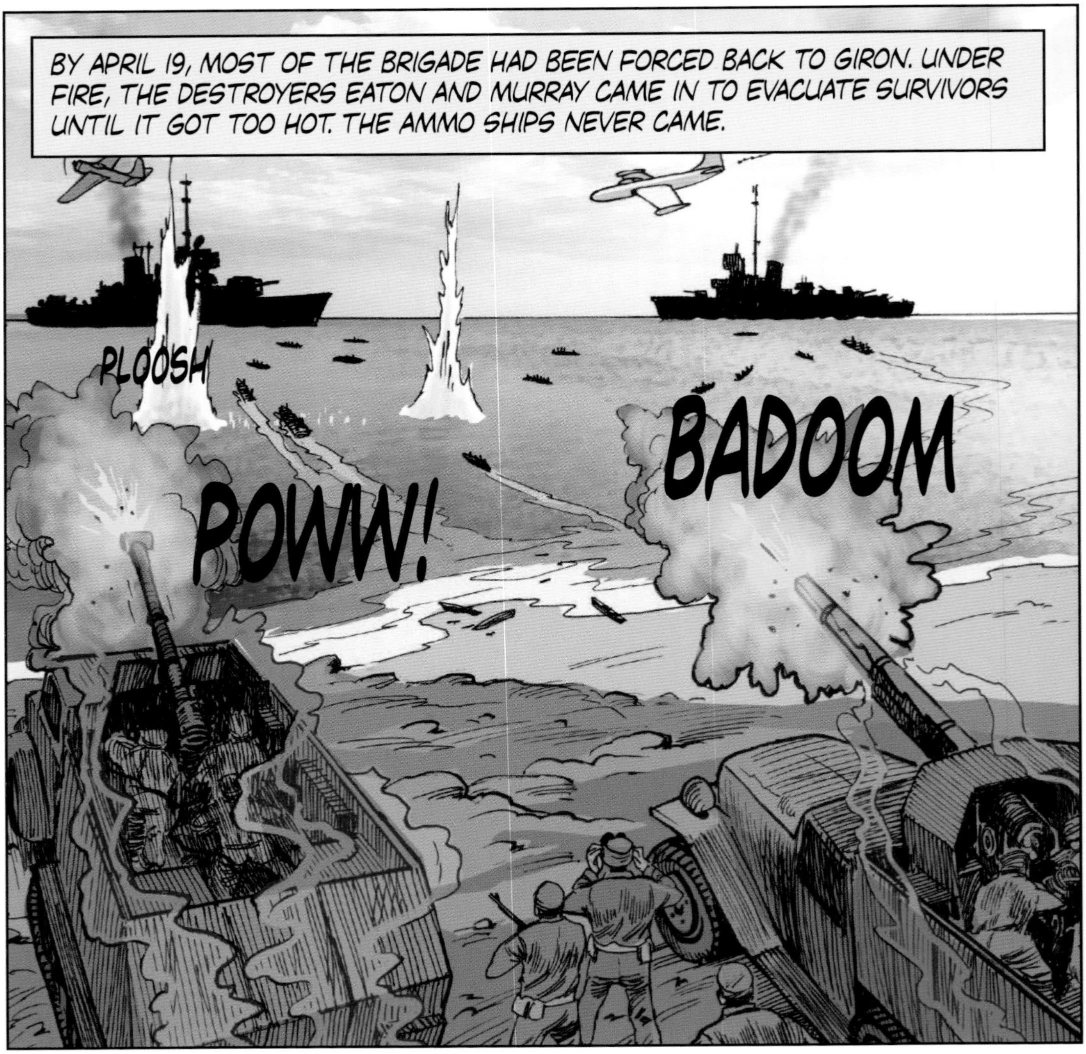
BY APRIL 19, MOST OF THE BRIGADE HAD BEEN FORCED BACK TO GIRON. UNDER FIRE, THE DESTROYERS EATON AND MURRAY CAME IN TO EVACUATE SURVIVORS UNTIL IT GOT TOO HOT. THE AMMO SHIPS NEVER CAME.
PLOOSH
POWW!
BADOOM

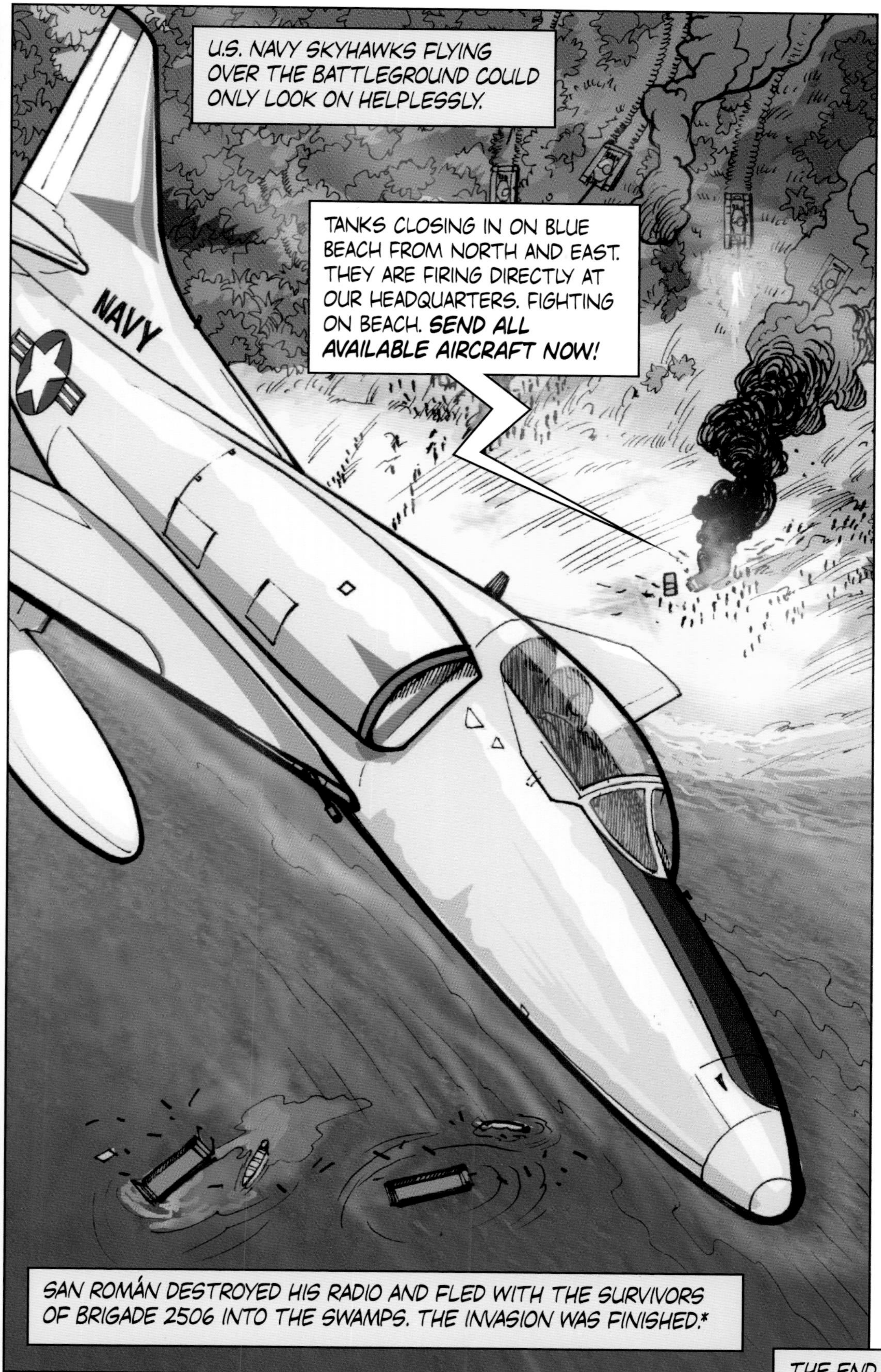
U.S. NAVY SKYHAWKS FLYING OVER THE BATTLEGROUND COULD ONLY LOOK ON HELPLESSLY.
TANKS CLOSING IN ON BLUE BEACH FROM NORTH AND EAST. THEY ARE FIRING DIRECTLY AT OUR HEADQUARTERS. FIGHTING ON BEACH. SEND ALL AVAILABLE AIRCRAFT NOW!
NAVY
SAN ROMÁN DESTROYED HIS RADIO AND FLED WITH THE SURVIVORS OF BRIGADE 2506 INTO THE SWAMPS. THE INVASION WAS FINISHED.*

THE END

*FOR A FULLER ACCOUNT OF WHAT WENT WRONG, SEE PAGE 6.

THE CUBAN MISSILE CRISIS, 1962

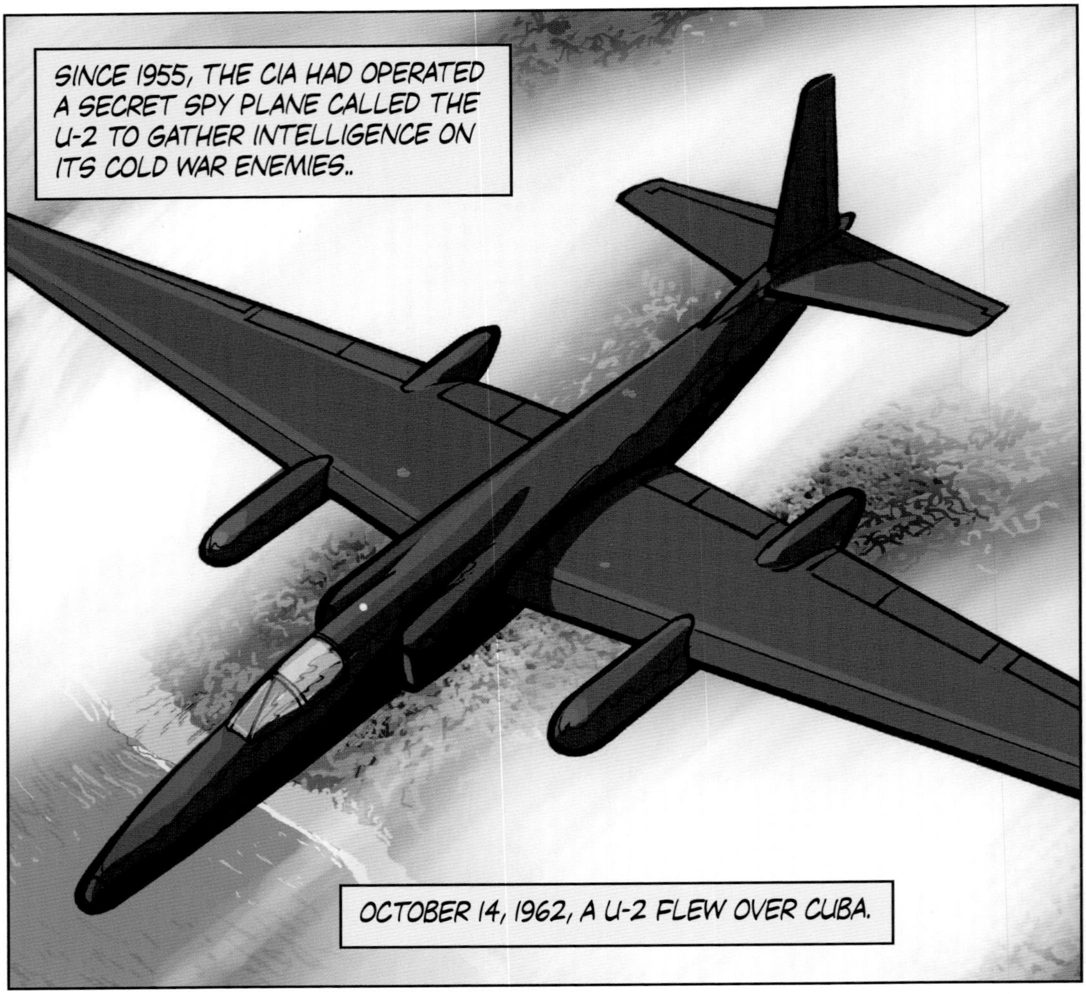
SINCE 1955, THE CIA HAD OPERATED A SECRET SPY PLANE CALLED THE U-2 TO GATHER INTELLIGENCE ON ITS COLD WAR ENEMIES..
OCTOBER 14, 1962, A U-2 FLEW OVER CUBA.

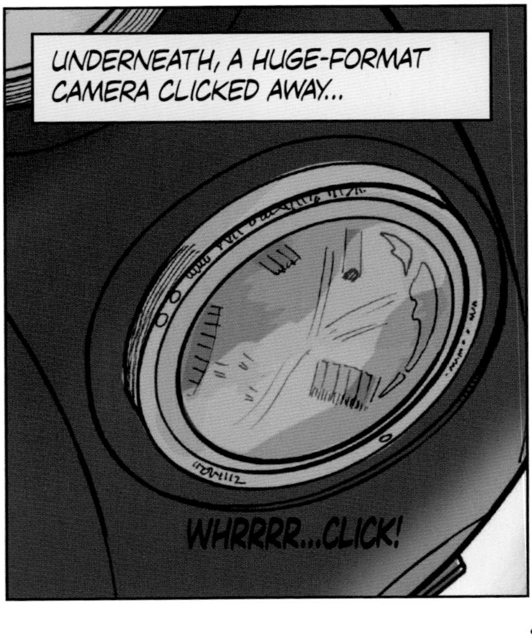
UNDERNEATH, A HUGE-FORMAT CAMERA CLICKED AWAY...
WHRRRR...CLICK!

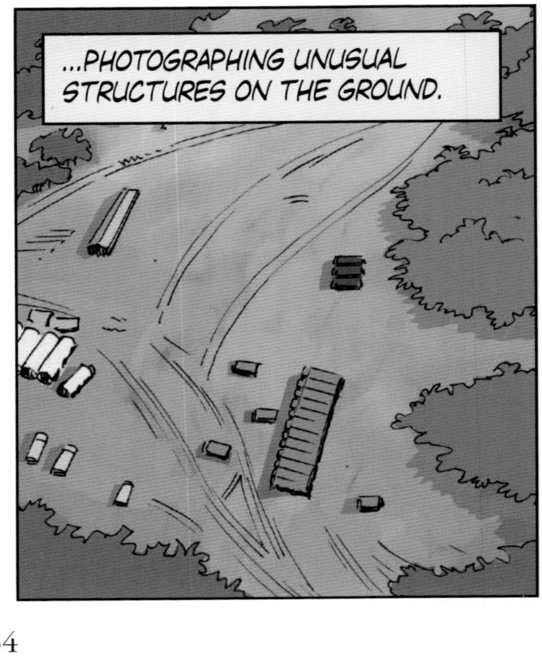
...PHOTOGRAPHING UNUSUAL STRUCTURES ON THE GROUND.

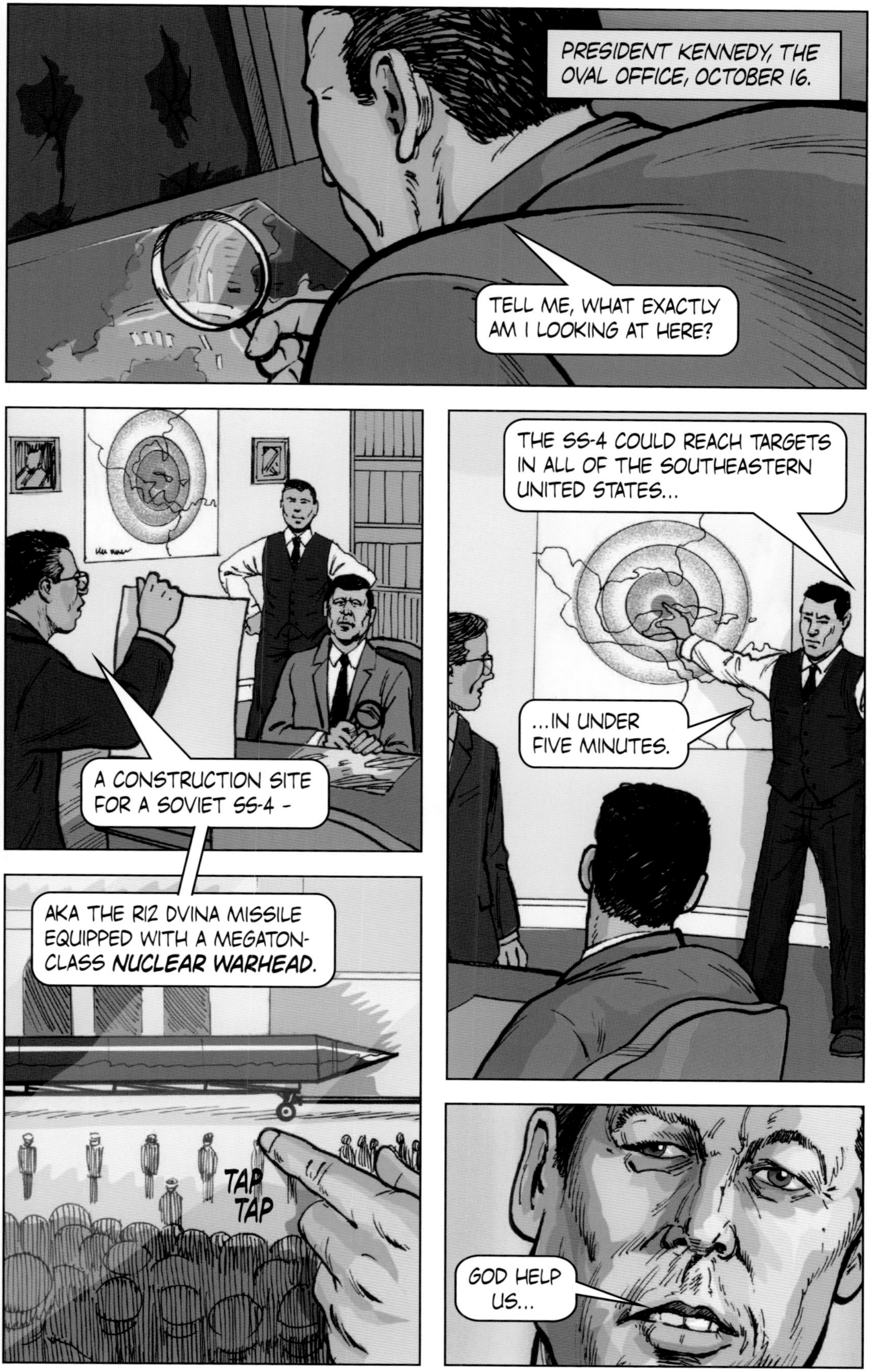
PRESIDENT KENNEDY, THE OVAL OFFICE, OCTOBER 16.
TELL ME, WHAT EXACTLY AM I LOOKING AT HERE?
A CONSTRUCTION SITE FOR A SOVIET SS-4 -
AKA THE R12 DVINA MISSILE EQUIPPED WITH A MEGATON-CLASS **NUCLEAR WARHEAD.**
TAP TAP
THE SS-4 COULD REACH TARGETS IN ALL OF THE SOUTHEASTERN UNITED STATES...
...IN UNDER FIVE MINUTES.
GOD HELP US...

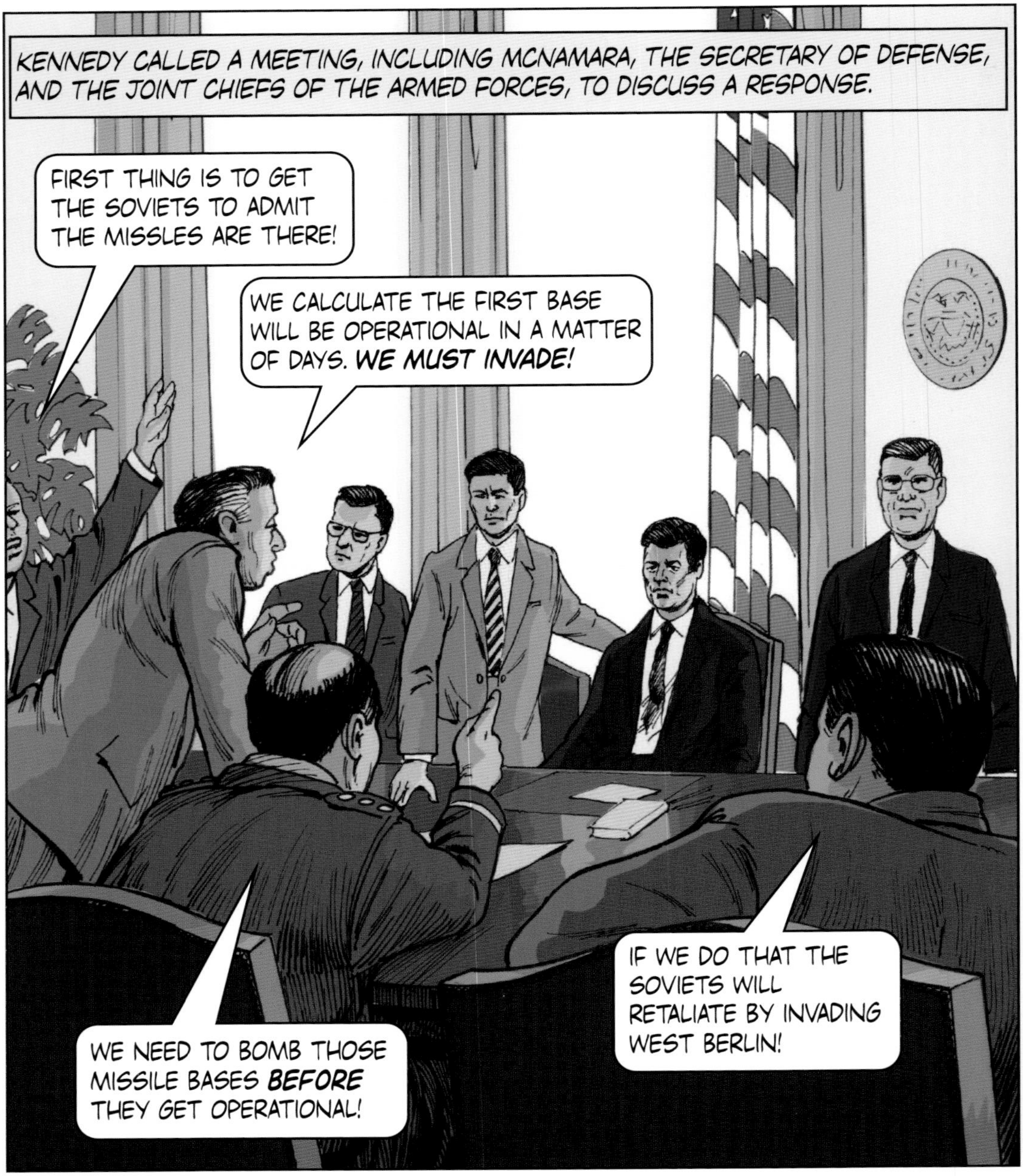
KENNEDY CALLED A MEETING, INCLUDING MCNAMARA, THE SECRETARY OF DEFENSE, AND THE JOINT CHIEFS OF THE ARMED FORCES, TO DISCUSS A RESPONSE.
FIRST THING IS TO GET THE SOVIETS TO ADMIT THE MISSLES ARE THERE!
WE CALCULATE THE FIRST BASE WILL BE OPERATIONAL IN A MATTER OF DAYS. WE MUST INVADE!
WE NEED TO BOMB THOSE MISSILE BASES BEFORE THEY GET OPERATIONAL!
IF WE DO THAT THE SOVIETS WILL RETALIATE BY INVADING WEST BERLIN!

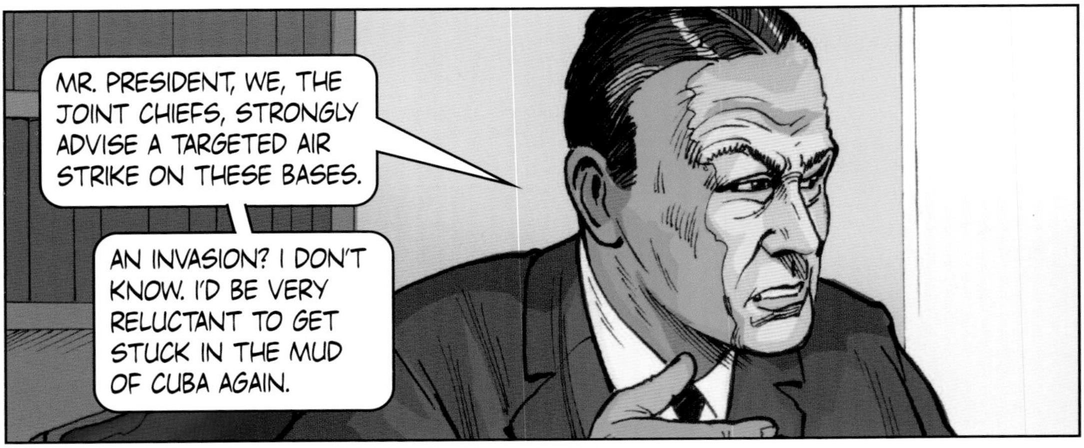
MR. PRESIDENT, WE, THE JOINT CHIEFS, STRONGLY ADVISE A TARGETED AIR STRIKE ON THESE BASES.
AN INVASION? I DON'T KNOW. I'D BE VERY RELUCTANT TO GET STUCK IN THE MUD OF CUBA AGAIN.

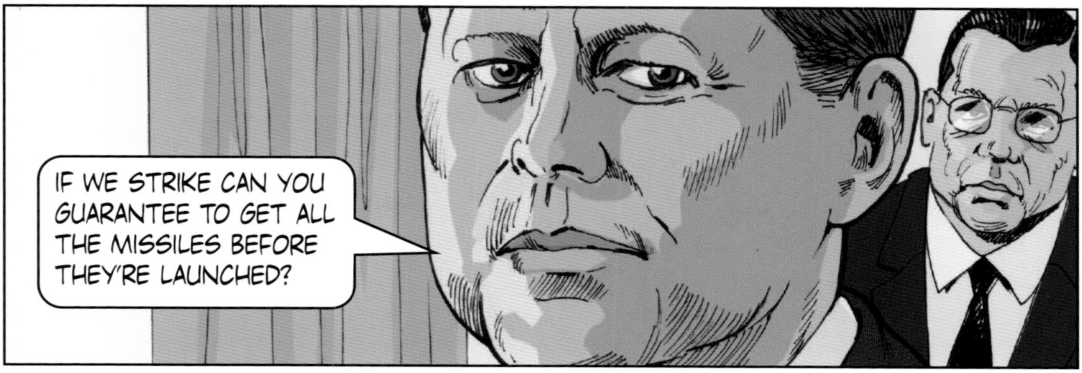
IF WE STRIKE CAN YOU GUARANTEE TO GET ALL THE MISSILES BEFORE THEY'RE LAUNCHED?

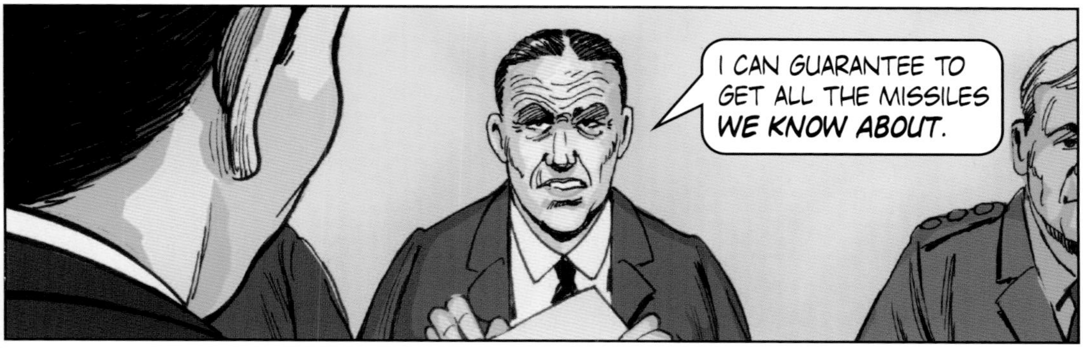
I CAN GUARANTEE TO GET ALL THE MISSILES **WE KNOW ABOUT**.

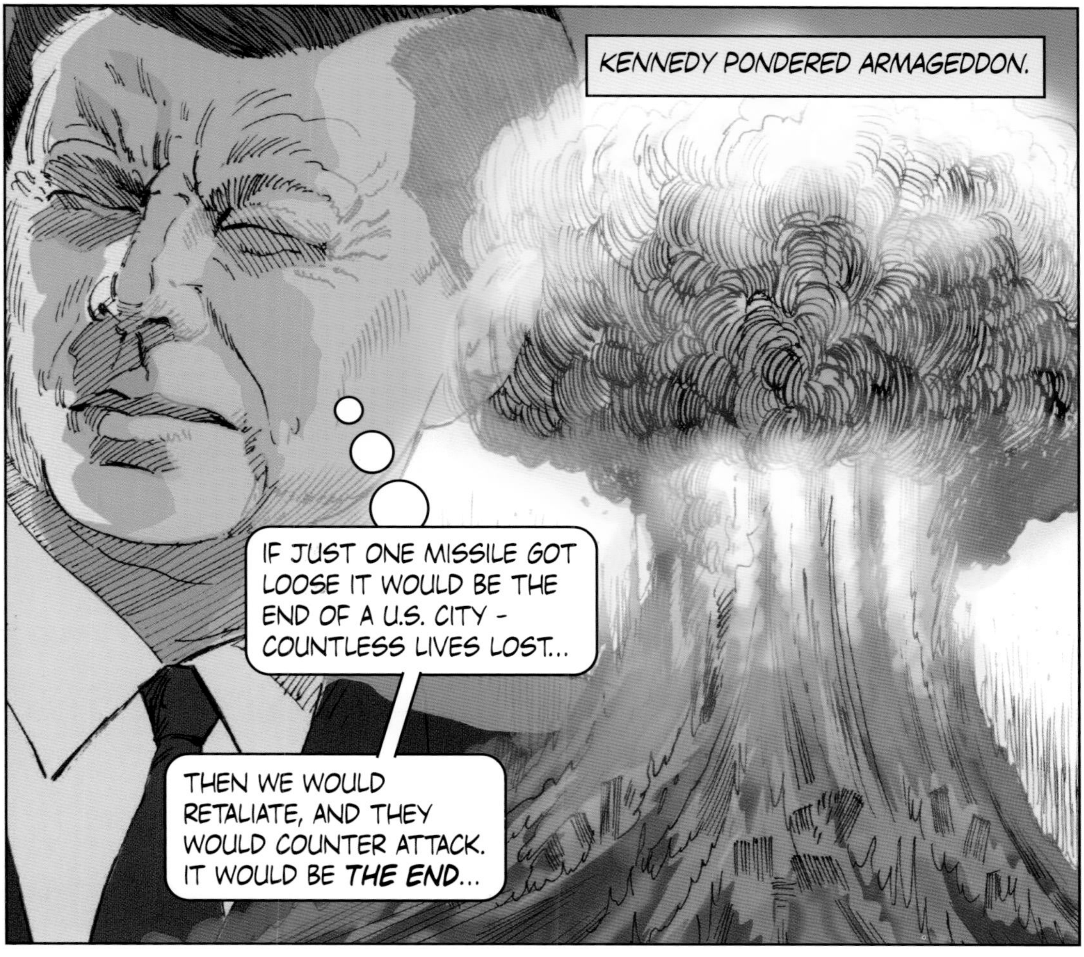
KENNEDY PONDERED ARMAGEDDON.
IF JUST ONE MISSILE GOT LOOSE IT WOULD BE THE END OF A U.S. CITY - COUNTLESS LIVES LOST...
THEN WE WOULD RETALIATE, AND THEY WOULD COUNTER ATTACK. IT WOULD BE **THE END**...

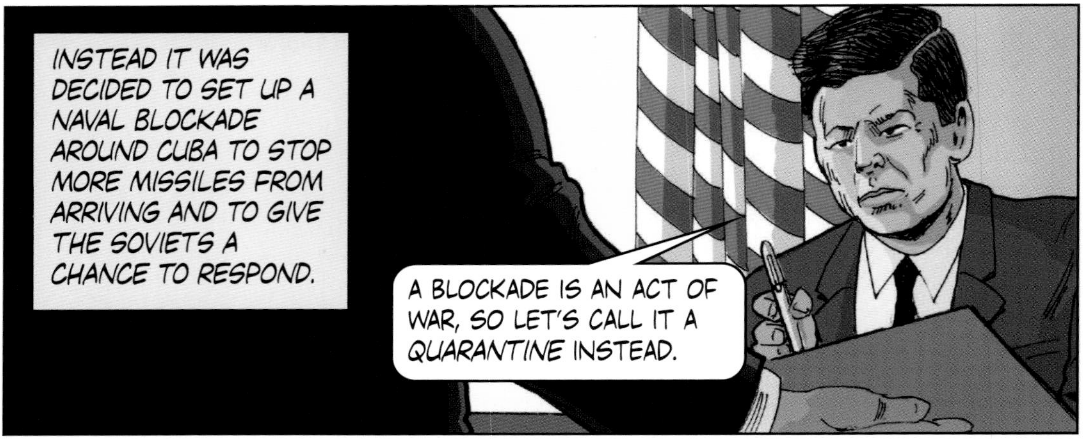
INSTEAD IT WAS DECIDED TO SET UP A NAVAL BLOCKADE AROUND CUBA TO STOP MORE MISSILES FROM ARRIVING AND TO GIVE THE SOVIETS A CHANCE TO RESPOND.
A BLOCKADE IS AN ACT OF WAR, SO LET'S CALL IT A *QUARANTINE* INSTEAD.

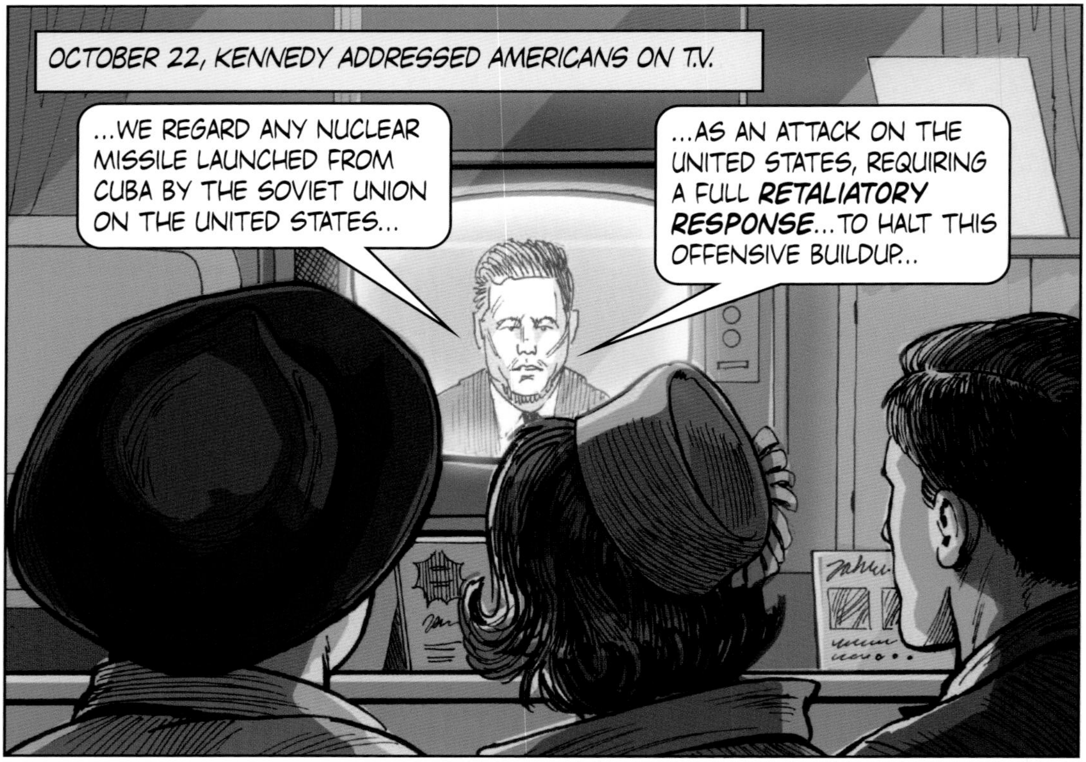
OCTOBER 22, KENNEDY ADDRESSED AMERICANS ON T.V.
...WE REGARD ANY NUCLEAR MISSILE LAUNCHED FROM CUBA BY THE SOVIET UNION ON THE UNITED STATES...
...AS AN ATTACK ON THE UNITED STATES, REQUIRING A FULL ***RETALIATORY RESPONSE***...TO HALT THIS OFFENSIVE BUILDUP...

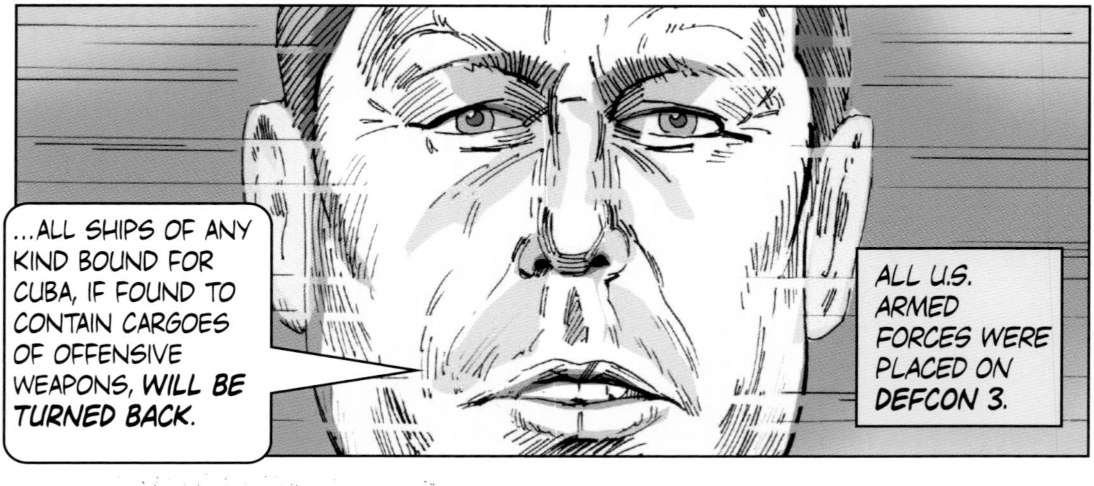
...ALL SHIPS OF ANY KIND BOUND FOR CUBA, IF FOUND TO CONTAIN CARGOES OF OFFENSIVE WEAPONS, ***WILL BE TURNED BACK.***
ALL U.S. ARMED FORCES WERE PLACED ON ***DEFCON 3.***

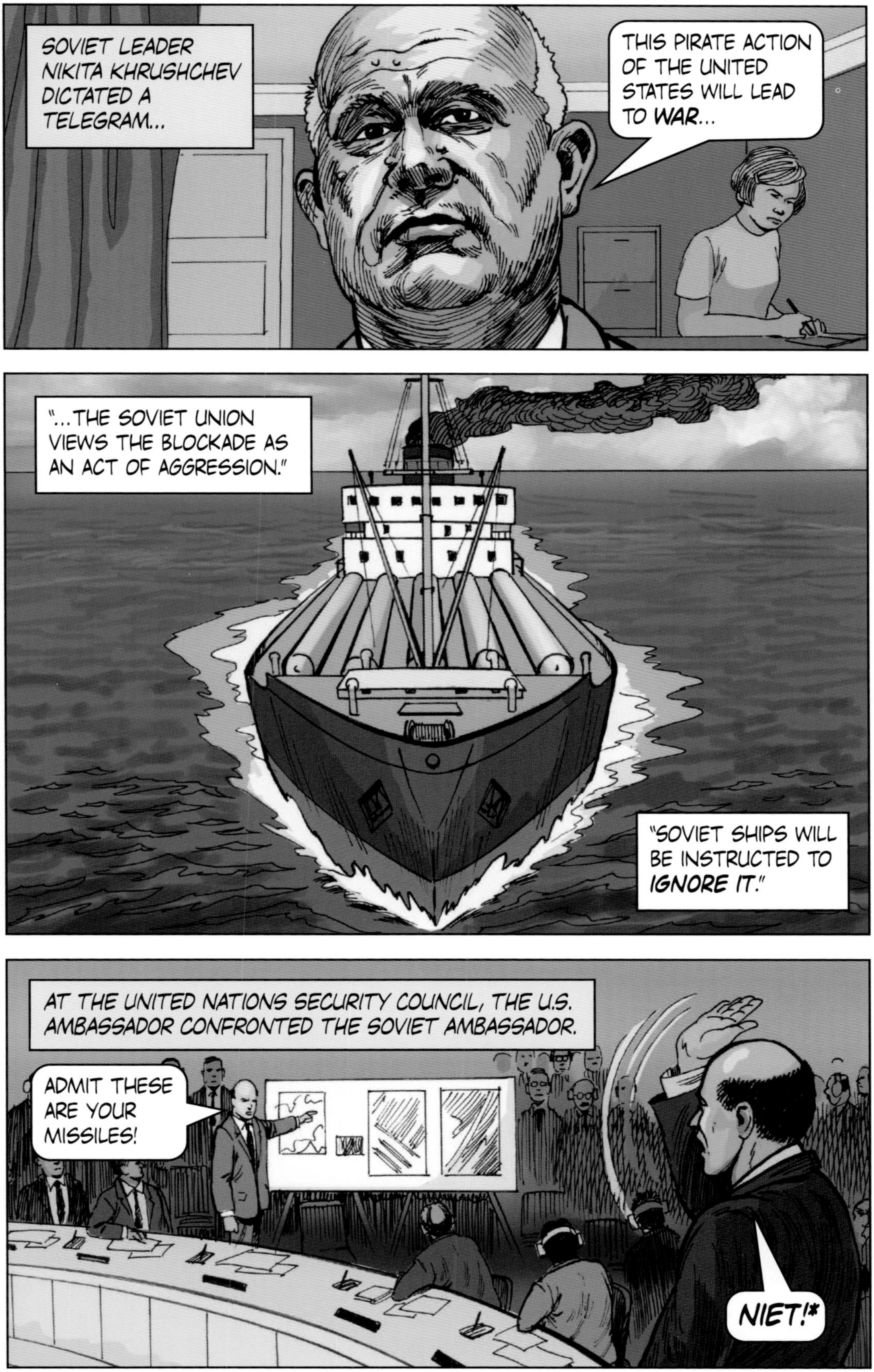
SOVIET LEADER NIKITA KHRUSHCHEV DICTATED A TELEGRAM...
THIS PIRATE ACTION OF THE UNITED STATES WILL LEAD TO **WAR**...
"...THE SOVIET UNION VIEWS THE BLOCKADE AS AN ACT OF AGGRESSION."
"SOVIET SHIPS WILL BE INSTRUCTED TO **IGNORE IT**."
AT THE UNITED NATIONS SECURITY COUNCIL, THE U.S. AMBASSADOR CONFRONTED THE SOVIET AMBASSADOR.
ADMIT THESE ARE YOUR MISSILES!
NIET!*

*NEVER

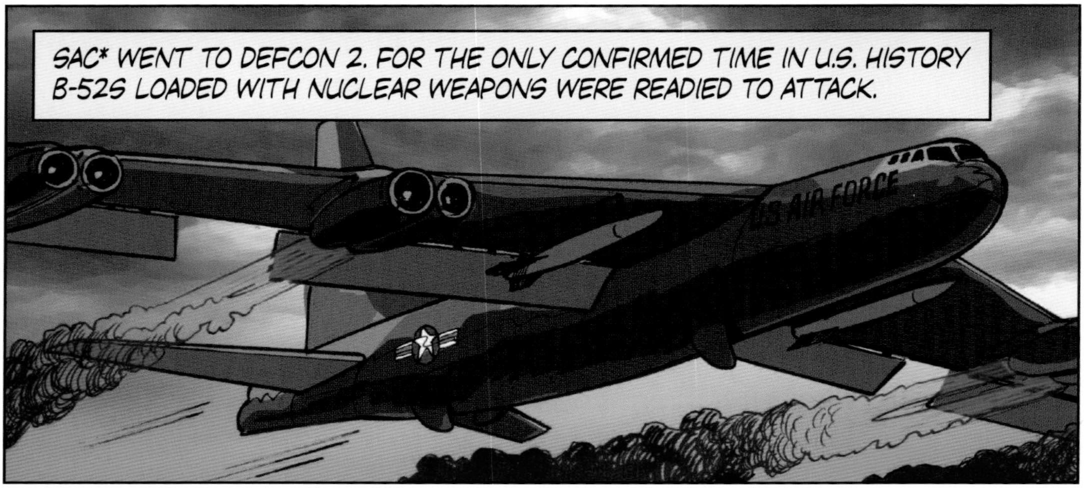
SAC* WENT TO DEFCON 2. FOR THE ONLY CONFIRMED TIME IN U.S. HISTORY B-52S LOADED WITH NUCLEAR WEAPONS WERE READIED TO ATTACK.
U.S. AIR FORCE

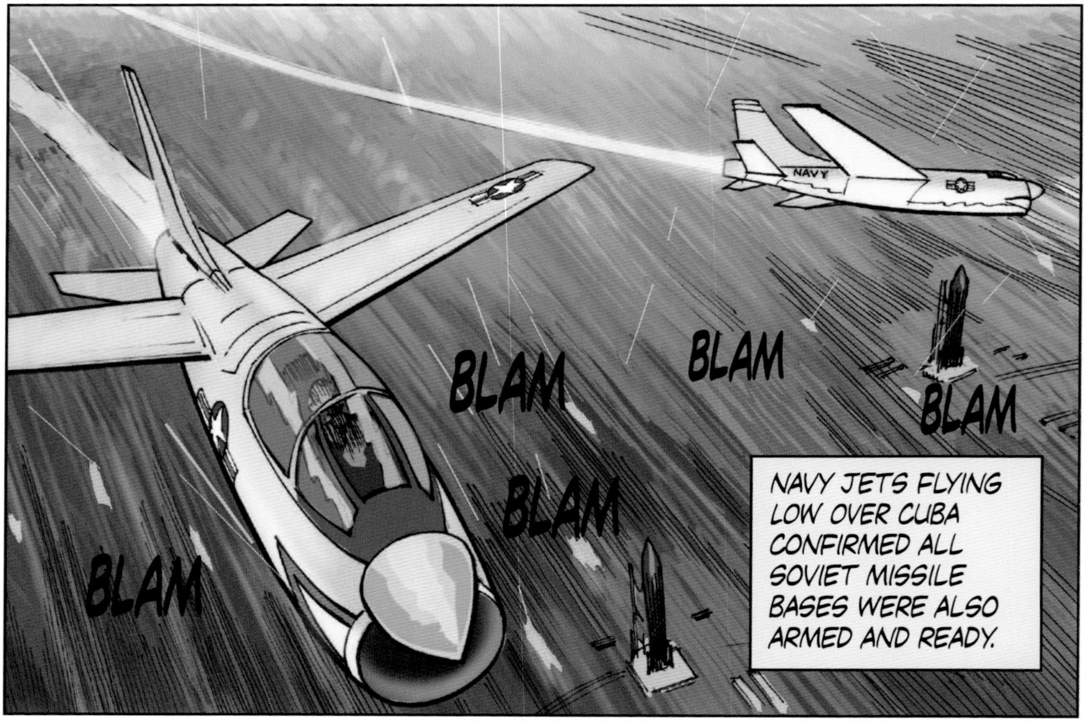
NAVY
BLAM
BLAM
BLAM
BLAM
BLAM
NAVY JETS FLYING LOW OVER CUBA CONFIRMED ALL SOVIET MISSILE BASES WERE ALSO ARMED AND READY.

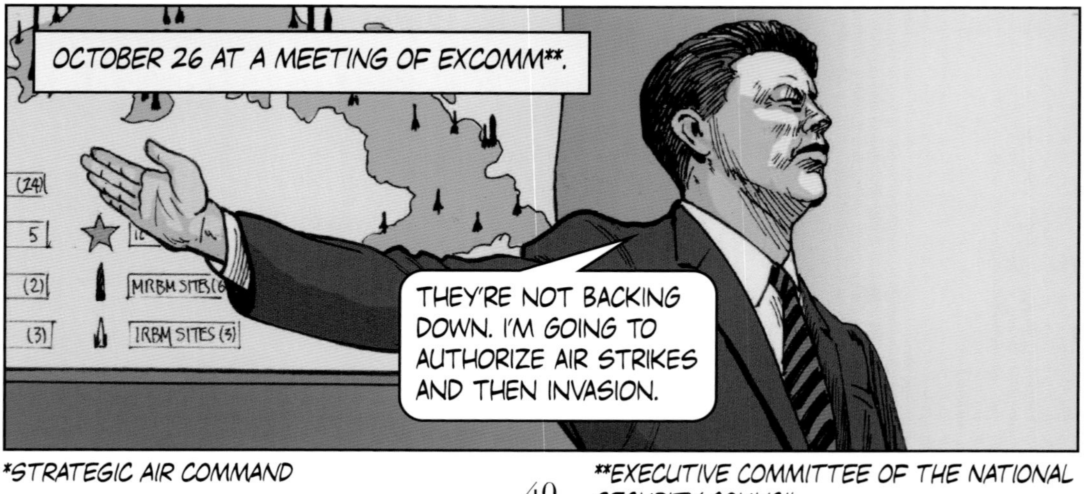
OCTOBER 26 AT A MEETING OF EXCOMM**.
(24)
5
(2)
(3)
IRBM SITES (3)
THEY'RE NOT BACKING DOWN. I'M GOING TO AUTHORIZE AIR STRIKES AND THEN INVASION.

*STRATEGIC AIR COMMAND

**EXECUTIVE COMMITTEE OF THE NATIONAL SECURITY COUNCIL

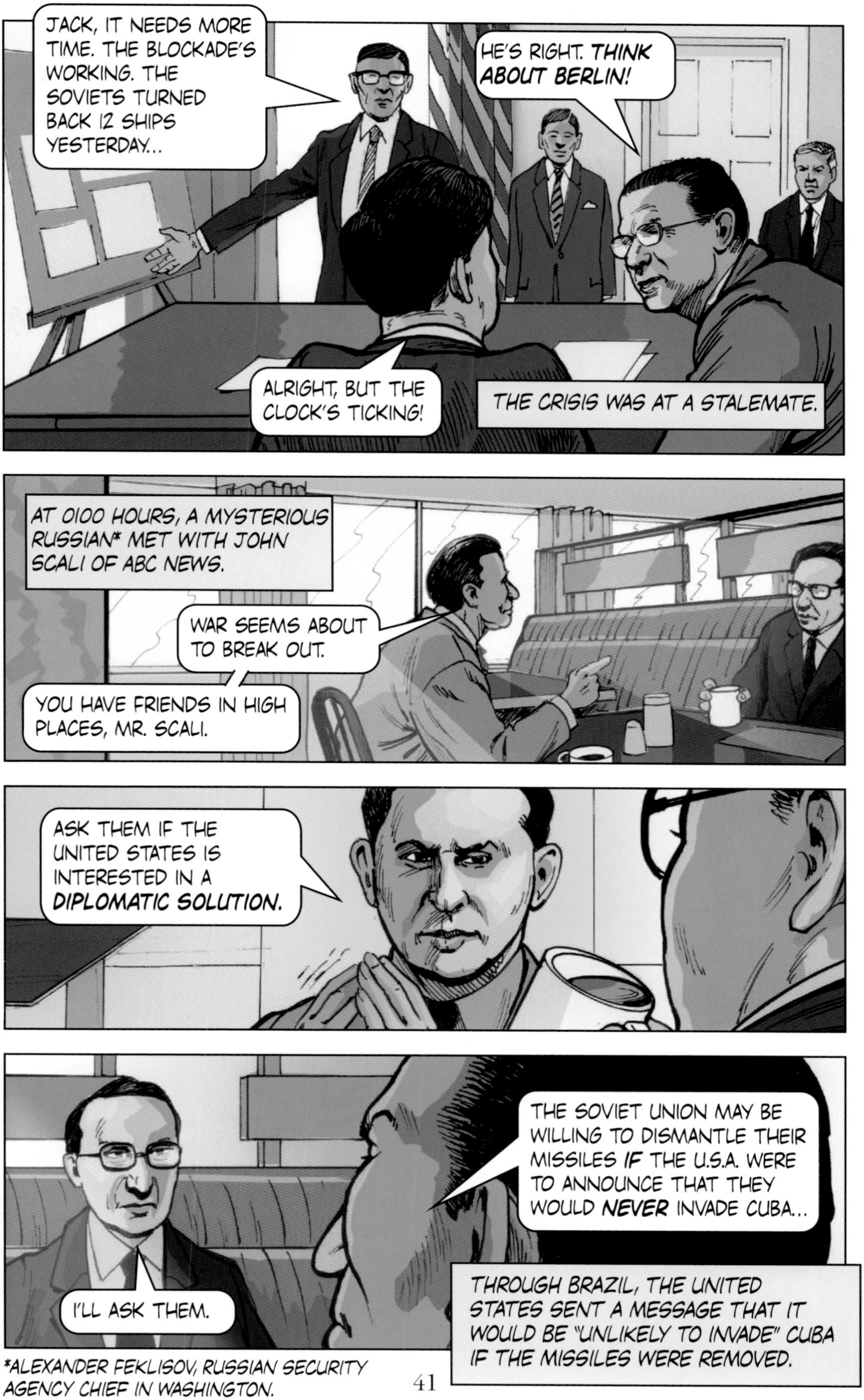
JACK, IT NEEDS MORE TIME. THE BLOCKADE'S WORKING. THE SOVIETS TURNED BACK 12 SHIPS YESTERDAY...
HE'S RIGHT. **THINK ABOUT BERLIN!**
ALRIGHT, BUT THE CLOCK'S TICKING!
THE CRISIS WAS AT A STALEMATE.
AT 0100 HOURS, A MYSTERIOUS RUSSIAN* MET WITH JOHN SCALI OF ABC NEWS.
WAR SEEMS ABOUT TO BREAK OUT.
YOU HAVE FRIENDS IN HIGH PLACES, MR. SCALI.
ASK THEM IF THE UNITED STATES IS INTERESTED IN A **DIPLOMATIC SOLUTION.**
THE SOVIET UNION MAY BE WILLING TO DISMANTLE THEIR MISSILES **IF** THE U.S.A. WERE TO ANNOUNCE THAT THEY WOULD **NEVER** INVADE CUBA...
I'LL ASK THEM.
THROUGH BRAZIL, THE UNITED STATES SENT A MESSAGE THAT IT WOULD BE "UNLIKELY TO INVADE" CUBA IF THE MISSILES WERE REMOVED.

*ALEXANDER FEKLISOV, RUSSIAN SECURITY AGENCY CHIEF IN WASHINGTON.

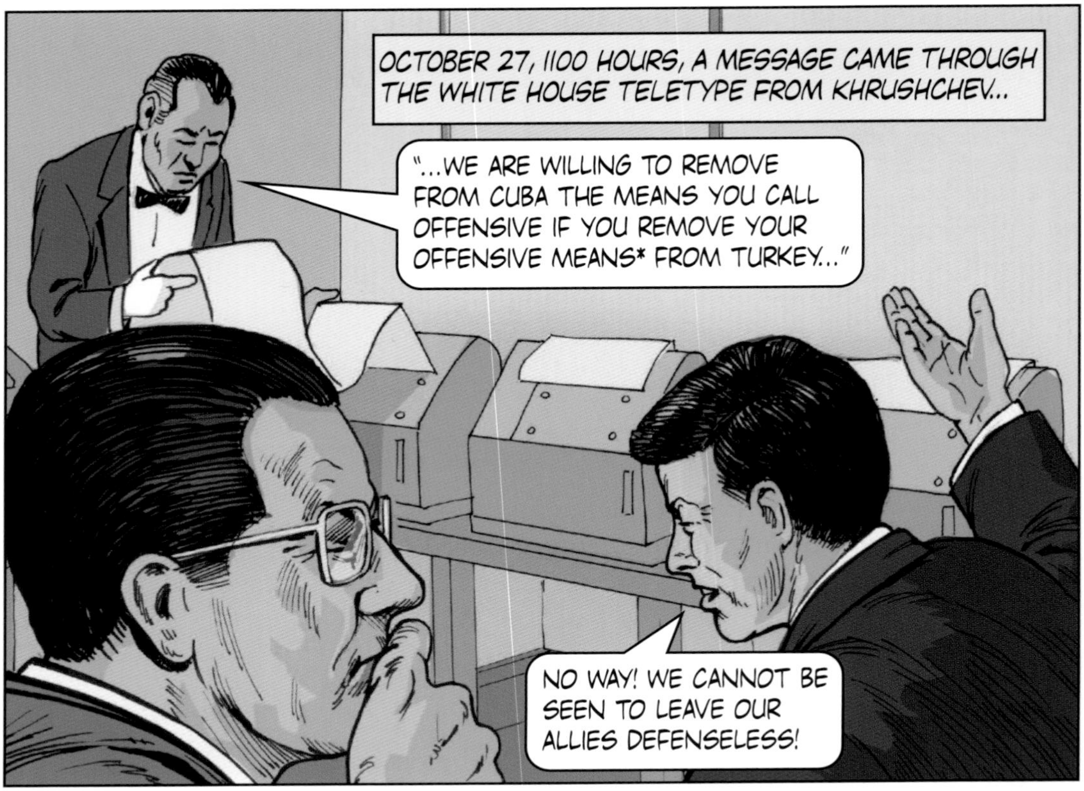
OCTOBER 27, 1100 HOURS, A MESSAGE CAME THROUGH THE WHITE HOUSE TELETYPE FROM KHRUSHCHEV...
"...WE ARE WILLING TO REMOVE FROM CUBA THE MEANS YOU CALL OFFENSIVE IF YOU REMOVE YOUR OFFENSIVE MEANS* FROM TURKEY..."
NO WAY! WE CANNOT BE SEEN TO LEAVE OUR ALLIES DEFENSELESS!

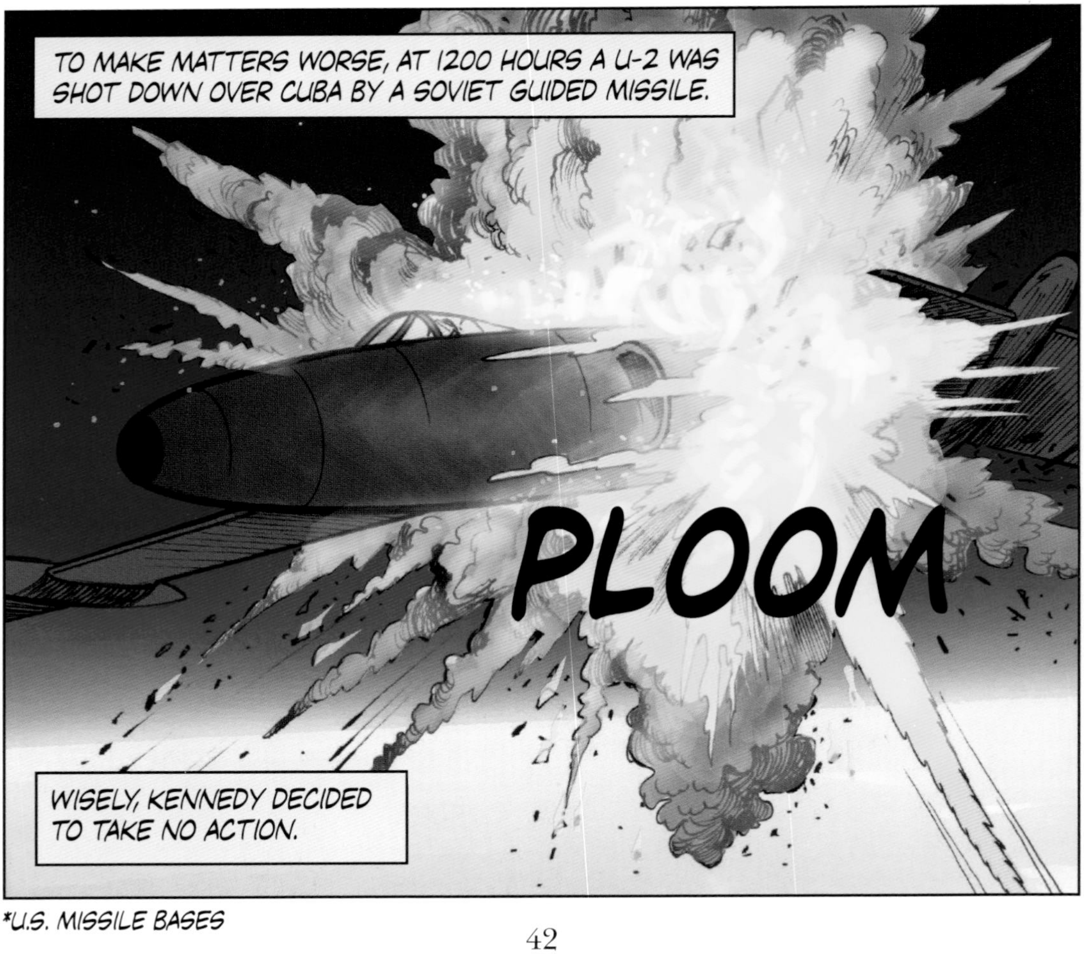
TO MAKE MATTERS WORSE, AT 1200 HOURS A U-2 WAS SHOT DOWN OVER CUBA BY A SOVIET GUIDED MISSILE.
PLOOM
WISELY, KENNEDY DECIDED TO TAKE NO ACTION.

*U.S. MISSILE BASES

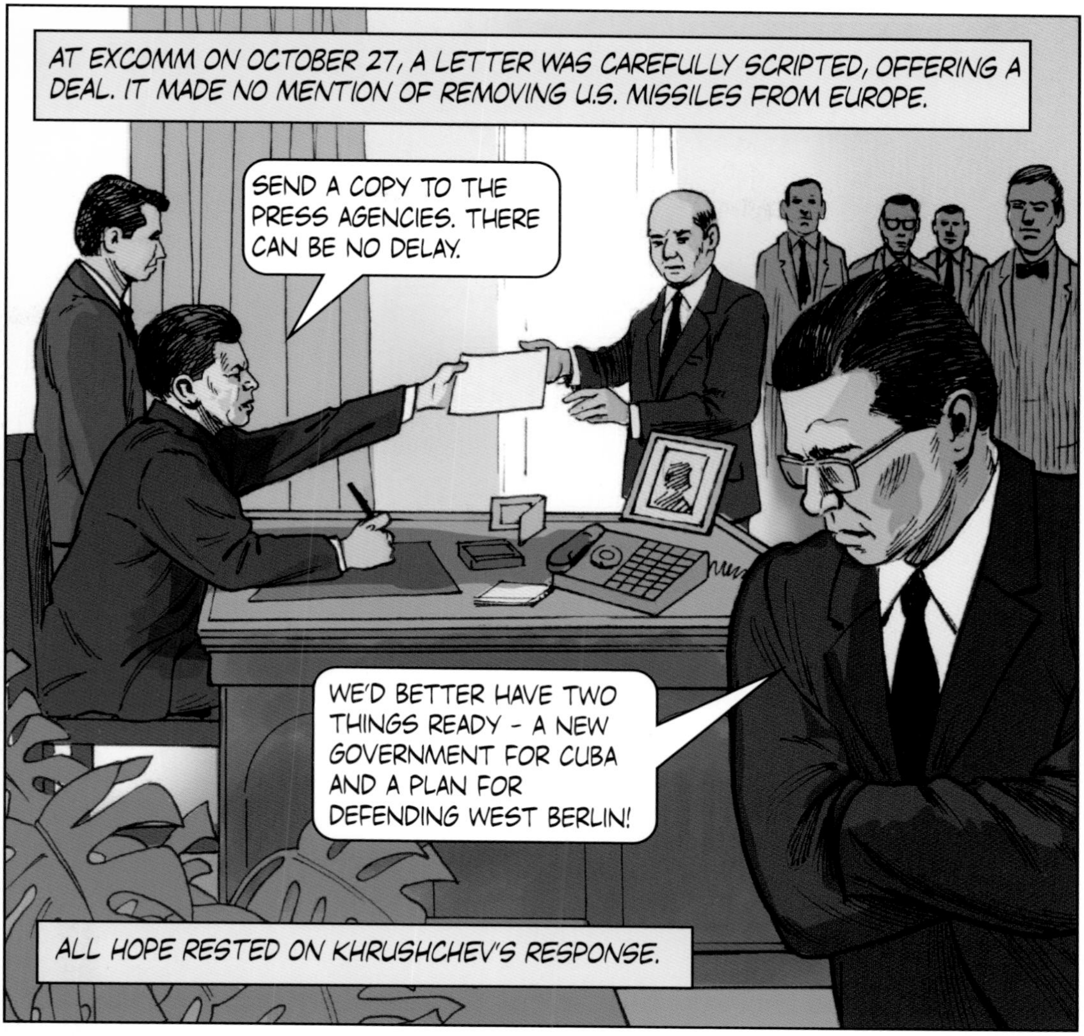
AT EXCOMM ON OCTOBER 27, A LETTER WAS CAREFULLY SCRIPTED, OFFERING A DEAL. IT MADE NO MENTION OF REMOVING U.S. MISSILES FROM EUROPE.
SEND A COPY TO THE PRESS AGENCIES. THERE CAN BE NO DELAY.
WE'D BETTER HAVE TWO THINGS READY - A NEW GOVERNMENT FOR CUBA AND A PLAN FOR DEFENDING WEST BERLIN!
ALL HOPE RESTED ON KHRUSHCHEV'S RESPONSE.

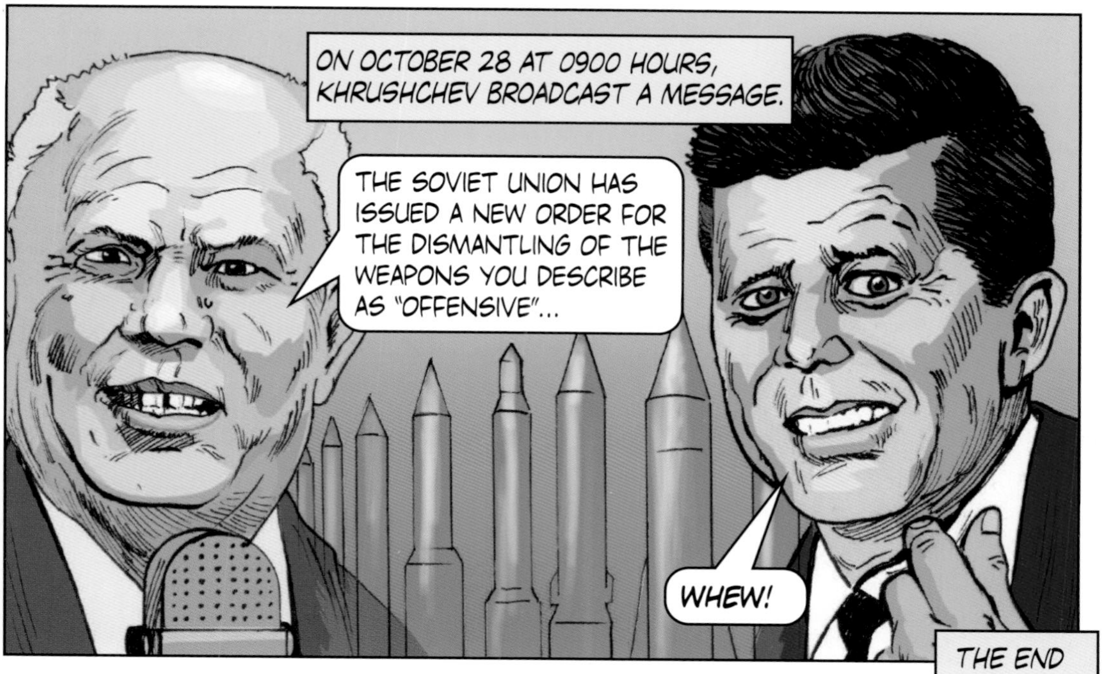
ON OCTOBER 28 AT 0900 HOURS, KHRUSHCHEV BROADCAST A MESSAGE.
THE SOVIET UNION HAS ISSUED A NEW ORDER FOR THE DISMANTLING OF THE WEAPONS YOU DESCRIBE AS "OFFENSIVE"...
WHEW!
THE END

COLD WAR RESOLUTIONS

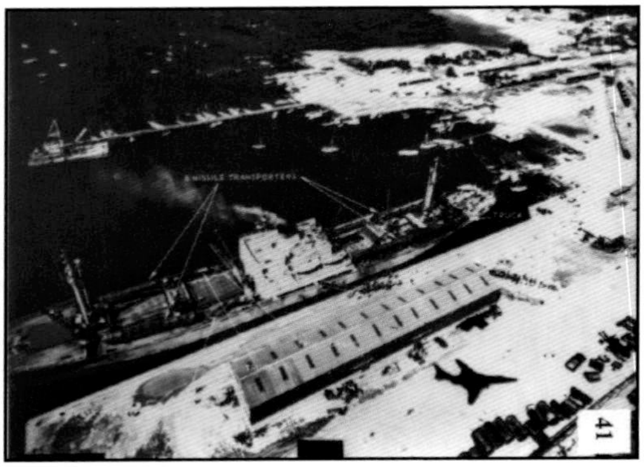

A CIA aerial photograph shows Soviet missiles being removed from Cuba, in November, 1962.

Kennedy's handling of the Cuban Missile Crisis was seen as a victory for an administration still tarnished by the Bay of Pigs disaster. The Cubans felt betrayed but the Soviets were happy—they had won a secret concession from the United States.

BACK DOOR TRADE-OFF

As far as the public was aware, the Cuban Missile Crisis had ended when the United States promised never to invade Cuba in return for a Soviet withdrawal. Secretly, the United States did agree to dismantle all U.S. Jupiter and Thor missile bases in Turkey and Italy. What the Soviets did not know was that these missiles had already become obsolete—replaced by Polaris ICBMs that could be launched by submarine from anywhere in the world. The settlement also led to the creation of a "hotline" direct communications link between Washington and Moscow.

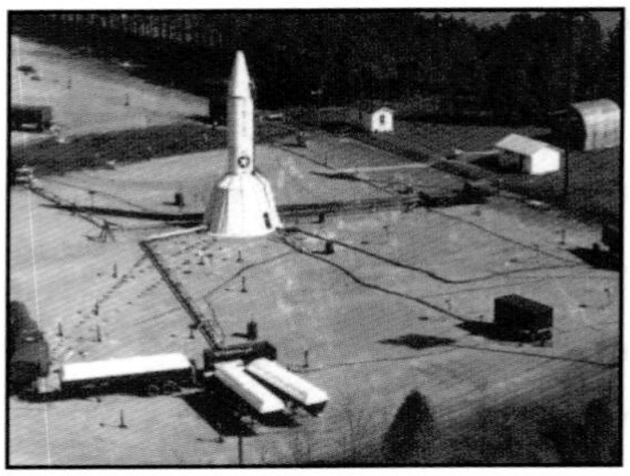

A Jupiter missile base

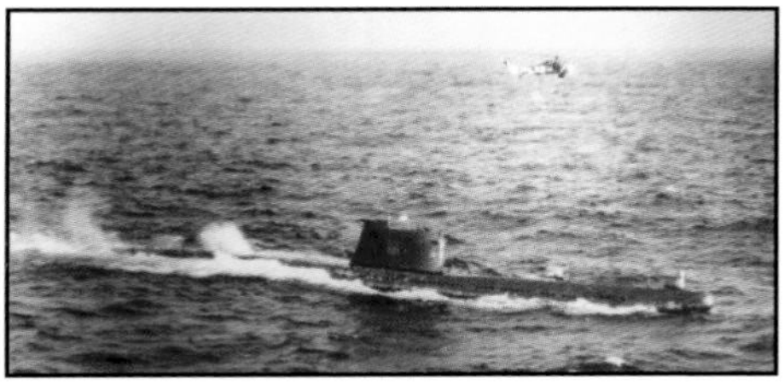

The most dangerous point of the crisis came on October 26, when the USS Beale *dropped a small depth charge on a Soviet submarine B-59 that they didn't know had a nuclear torpedo. Enraged, the sub's captain ordered the torpedo armed before eventually calming down and surfacing.*

AS CLOSE AS IT CAME

In recent times it was discovered that, in addition to the 42 R12 missiles, the Soviets also had tactical nuclear warheads available for their artillery rockets and Il-28 long-range bomber aircraft stationed on Cuba.

Castro has said he was willing to use them on the United States if Cuba was invaded, even though the island itself would be destroyed in retaliation.

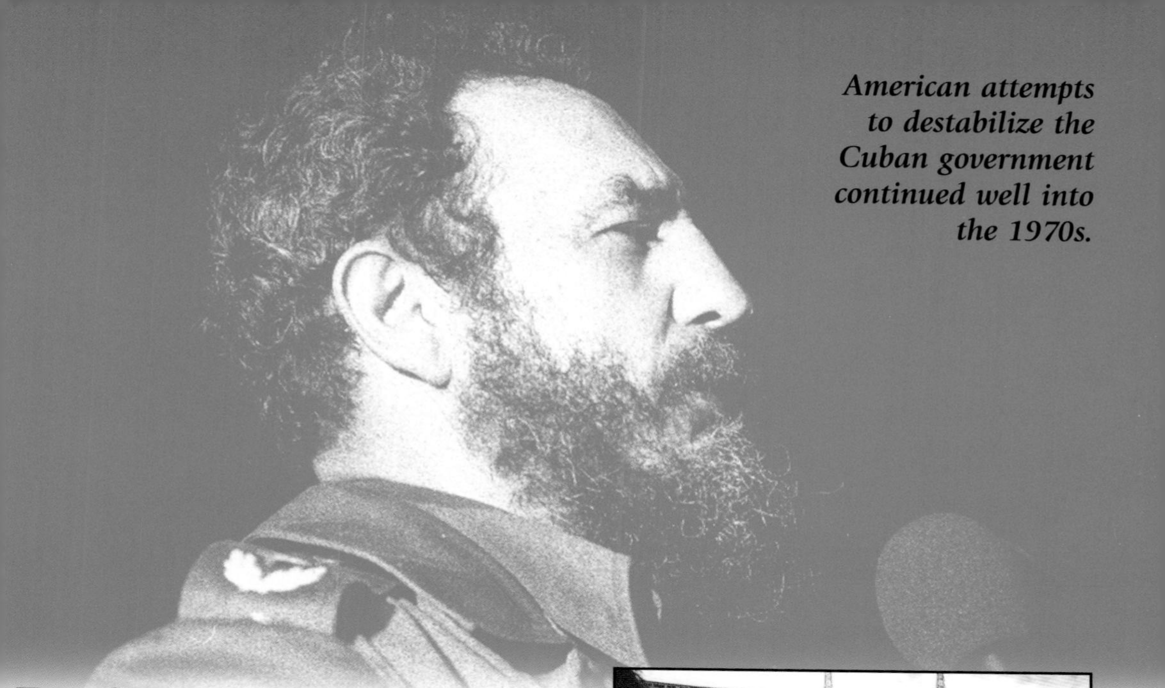

American attempts to destabilize the Cuban government continued well into the 1970s.

The Cuban Way

Dismayed at being a pawn in the Cold War confrontation between the superpowers, Castro nevertheless continued to develop his relationship with the Soviets, who carried on importing most of Cuba's sugar.

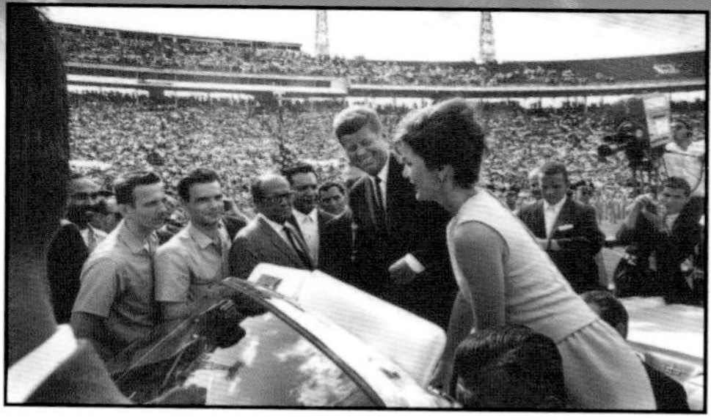

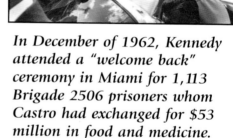

In December of 1962, Kennedy attended a "welcome back" ceremony in Miami for 1,113 Brigade 2506 prisoners whom Castro had exchanged for $53 million in food and medicine.

Guevara meanwhile had been trying to mastermind the economy, but his attempts to mobilize Cuban industry failed. Guevara was a soldier at heart, and he decided to try to export the Cuban revolutionary model to other oppressed nations. His actions in the Congo and Bolivia both failed, and the latter cost him his life.

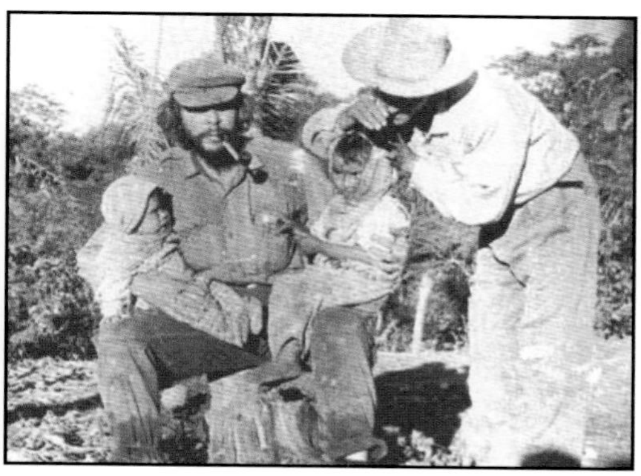

Guevara is shown here in 1967 in Bolivia, shortly before his death.

Castro made himself head of State in 1975, and Cuba supported a reasonable standard of living until the collapse of the Soviet Union in 1991. Hard times lay ahead, leading Castro to resurrect the image of Che Guevara—a symbol of revolutionary self-sacrifice, determination, and the spirit that had helped Cuba survive despite the American embargo, which is still in effect today.

GLOSSARY

A-bomb Atomic bomb, a devastating nuclear weapon

allies Nations that have an agreed alliance with each other for the benefit of all the countries that are members

amidships The middle part of a ship

ammunition Objects, such as bullets, that can be fired from guns

Armageddon A term used to refer to a possible end-of-the-world event

artillery rockets High caliber weapons used during battle that are equipped with rocket launchers instead of guns or mortars

barricade An obstacle put in place to stop an enemy from advancing

beachhead A position on an enemy shoreline captured by troops in advance of an invading force

blockade A military action that stops supplies and troops from entering or leaving an enemy country

brigade A smaller part or subdivision of an army that has a specific purpose

CIA Central Intelligence Agency—one of the principal intelligence-gathering agencies of the United States federal government

civilian A citizen who is not fighting in the army

Cold War A period of political tension from 1947 to 1990 during which communist countries led by the Soviet Union and democratic countries from the West led by the United States competed militarily. Each side tried to control or influence unstable countries around the world in an effort to spread their own styles of government.

column A long line of troops

communism A political philosophy that says everyone should be treated equally and all goods should be shared equally

counterrevolution An action to overthrow a government that was put in place when a different group overthrew the government before it

coup An overthrow of a government, usually by a group determined to replace it with another government, either civil or military

covert Not openly made or done

DEFCON A "defense readiness condition," or level of military alert, used to identify the severity of a threat to the United States

defectors People who leave one country or army to join an enemy

demoralized To be deprived of spirit or morale

destabilize To cause a government to be unable to operate as usual

dictator One person that rules a country or state with absolute power

embargo A government ban against trade with a particular country

exiles People forced by a situation to leave their country to live in another country

frogmen Divers trained in scuba diving or swimming underwater

garrison Where a group of soldiers is located, either to guard the position or to use it as a home base

guerrillas Forces not part of the regular army

ideologies Sets of beliefs that form the basis of political or economic systems

Marxist A person who follows a social and political philosophy of communism created by German philosopher Karl Marx

moderate A person whose political beliefs are not extreme

Molotov cocktail A fire bomb, usually made by hand

nuclear warhead Part of a missile that contains a nuclear-powered explosive

offensive A carefully planned military attack

pawn Someone or a thing being used by a greater force for its own ends

phosphorus grenade A quickly burning explosive that creates smoke

puppet A leader put in place and controlled by a foreign authority

radicalized Introduced a change in thinking, often political

repressed Controlled the actions and free speech of citizens by force

retaliatory Relating to an action taken in response to a similar action

stalemate A point in time when neither side in a game or conflict can make a move to win

tracer fire Chemical trails from ammunition that help shooters correct their aim

Members of EXCOMM attempt to resolve the Cuban Missile Crisis in 1962.

47

INDEX